"My goal as team leader of the Prayer Ministry Team is to lead the church body into being burdened for God's Kingdom. I truly believe your book to be one of the most exhaustive resources I have ever seen on praying the Word of God. I believe that God has equipped you for this time in the history of our nation."

Mary Lou Colquitt, Prayer Ministry Team Leader
First Baptist Church of Waxahachie, TX

"This book has changed my life! I now have confidence to pray in public, with my husband, and also my coworkers. Not only have I learned to pray, but I now know who I am in Jesus Christ. What a blessing to know who God is and what His plan is for my life!"

Valeria Johnson, Elder
Glad Tidings Church, Morehead City, NC

"Recently I was in a car accident and a friend of mine was injured as well. Throughout our long difficult recovery, she stayed so upbeat and positive. One day I asked how she was staying so strong in her faith. She told me about Praying in the Word of God, *'that one book that made her so happy!' I began to use the book and found that it has had an incredible impact on my daily relationship with the Lord."*

Barb Bodenner
Bella Vista Church, Rockford, MI

"What a panoramic quality my prayer life has now that I am using your book! My prayers have become far more focused on others. Now, instead of just thanking God for the privilege, honor, and gift of being able to breast-feed my daughter, I pray for other moms to have the same blessing of nourishing their babies in such a special way. Using your book has made my prayer time richer, more specific, more scripturally sound, more pleasing to Jesus and certainly more powerful! Lifting up many specific names makes me mindful to pray for them throughout the day. Praying for the lost has taken on a whole new meaning for me—how exciting!"

Wendy Tharrington
Englewood Baptist Church, Rocky Mt., NC

*If you remain in Me and My words remain in you,
ask whatever you wish, and it will be given you.*
John 15:7

"I have used many prayer guides, read books, and used scripture as I have sought to become an intercessor, but when I read Praying in the Word of God my entire life changed. This book is a well organized and designed plan on how to use the Word of God to pray for His will to be accomplished. This resource will help you become more effective in the greatest work of our Lord and His Kingdom—PRAYER!"

Steve Ellis, Executive Pastor
Siloam Baptist Church (SBC), Easley, SC

"I had been a pastor for twenty-five years, but until I got this book, I never really knew how to pray! This book has opened up a whole new world to me."

Del Roberts, Senior Pastor
Grace Community Church (AOG), Englewood, CO

"The most effective, comprehensive guide to prayer I have ever been able to offer my congregation. This Scripturally based tool assures praying in the will of God!"

John Barham, Senior Pastor
First United Methodist Church of Pinellas Park, FL

"How often I have felt so inadequate as I entered the throne room of almighty God! But now, since I started using Praying in the Word of God, *I come boldly to the throne of Grace and find mercy and grace to help me in my time of need. This author has done a marvelous job of organizing the Scriptures in such a way to make praying the will of God encouraging, understandable, and practical."*

Steve Sherwood, Senior Pastor
Fairview Baptist Church, Kokomo, IN

"Kathleen Grant's book is an indispensable tool to enhance you prayer life! This Bible-based prayer book will align your will with the heart of God and your prayers will become more comprehensive and purposeful. Praying in the Word of God *is helping our church become a people of prayer."*

Larry Orth, Pastor of Evangelism and Discipleship
Calvary Evangelical Free Church, Rochester, MN

PRAYING
IN THE
WORD OF GOD

ADVANCING CHRIST'S KINGDOM

KATHLEEN G. GRANT

PRAYER PARTNERS WITH GOD PUBLISHING
ENGLEWOOD, CO

Scripture (and Scripture quotations) taken from the HOLY BIBLE, NEW INTERNATIONAL VERSION R, NIV R. Copyright 1973, 1978, 1984 by International Bible Society. Used by permission of Zondervan Publishing House.

List of nations taken from *Operation World* copyright©2001 Patrick Johnstone and Jason Mandryk. Published by Paternoster Lifestyle, Carlisle, U.K. Permission granted. All rights reserved.

Maps obtained under license from Map Resources <mapresources.com>

Grant, Kathleen G.
    Praying in the word of God : advancing Chirst's
kingdom / Kathleen G. Grant
    p. cm.
    ISBN: 0-9749684-0-4

    1. Prayer--Christianity. 2. Christian life.
3. Confession. I. Title.

BV210.3.G73 2004   248.3'2
                                    QBI33-2025

Prayer Partners With God Publishing
P.O. Box 9292
Englewood, CO 80111
(303) 781-6484
(303) 781-6585 Fax
www.PrayerPartnersWithGod.com

Printed in the USA by Bethany Press International.

ACKNOWLEDGMENTS

This book is dedicated to the Lord Jesus Christ, who saved me out of darkness and brought me into His wonderful light! It is for His glory and honor and for the advancement of His Kingdom that this book was written.

I thank Him for so many people who were responsible for my salvation: for my great-great grandmother on my father's side who was a profoundly devout Christian for her prayers, for the nuns in the hospital in Rome, Italy, who told me of Jesus in 1951 when my mother was hospitalized for four months and almost died, and for President Jimmy Carter, whose public witness of the gospel caused me to seek the Lord Jesus Christ. Most of all, I thank God for my twin sister, Christina Free, who prayed and witnessed to me for six and a half years before I came to Christ and my brother, Andrew Free, who sent me a seventy-nine page letter telling me everything he could think of to convince me that Jesus is Lord and Savior. The day that I received that letter, I gave my life to Christ.

To those who helped me grow, I give my love and my thanks. I think of Pastor Ray and Jan Dupont who reached out to Paul and me with such love in the first year of our salvation. Also, I thank Sharon Barnes who prayed with me for hours at a time in those early months! I am most grateful for the book, *The Adversary*, by Dr. Mark Bubeck, because it is filled with doctrinal prayers that revealed to me my position in Christ and taught me to pray the Word of God. I will always think of Dr. Bubeck as my spiritual father! Without his prayers, I would not be the author of this book. Finally, I think of Ruth Zigler, now with the Lord, who was the mightiest woman of prayer I have ever known and who powerfully validated the call of prayer on my life.

While I do not believe in the doctrine of entire sanctification, I am grateful for Andrew Murray's books because of how they stimulated me to seek to live wholly for God. His books on prayer remain some of my favorites. But the author whose book on prayer has remained the most important of all to me is S.D. Gordon. His book, *Quiet Talks on Prayer,* encouraged me to continue in prayer when I was quite alone and had no support.

My thanks go to those who have been a part of this book's development through the years: to Dave Bennett, director of evangelism at the Missouri Baptist Convention, and Carla Martin, his secretary, who helped distribute it in its early stages and to Murray Fisher, of Longwood Communications, who helped me continue its development.

I am especially grateful to Sharon Castlen of Integrated Book Marketing for her wisdom and tact in guiding me in all phases of this book's development and distribution, to Faithe Finley of Master Design Ministries who edited and produced the book for me, and to Larry Carpenter, Dave Troutman, and all the gang at FaithWorks, the only book distributor for small Christian publishing companies, for their work in distributing it to the trade.

My deepest gratitude goes to my most wonderful, husband, Paul, who has always given me his full support and guidance through the years this book was being written. If he had not joined me in this ministry of prayer that has come to mean so much to both of us, this book would never have been published. He has been so humble, so proud of me, so constant in his love and devotion to me and to the "call" of prayer in my life, that there simply isn't anyway to thank him enough! He is the kindest and most supportive husband a woman could have. Whenever I read the word "servant" in the Bible, I think of him. He has laid down his life for me, our ministry, and our children. Because he has joined me in creating and giving our prayer seminars, churches are willing to have us come to impact the whole church, both men and women.

A special "thank you" goes to Jason, our dear son, who has put up with our being gone for many weekends over the years as we traveled around the country giving our prayer seminars. He has always "held down the fort" with great faithfulness, taken care of our dog "Mr. Bear", and enabled us to be away without worries of any kind.

My eternal thanks go to Evangelist William Fay, author of *Share Jesus Without Fear*, for believing in me and my ministry of prayer. He has been a constant source of prayer, wisdom, and encouragement. No one could have a better friend and brother in Christ than he has been to us!

A Personal Note from Kathie

Dear Prayer Partner,

I commend you for being interested in enhancing your prayer life! It is wonderful that you are praying already and want to do more. I have noticed in my own relationship with the Lord, that whenever He is about to expand my walk with Him, He causes me to hunger for more! You may be feeling this way about your prayer life! You long to pray even more faithfully, purposefully and comprehensively for the things that concern Him and His Kingdom. You hunger to bear fruit for Him through prayer, claiming His promises and meeting His conditions for answered prayer. You believe that His Words are the key to everything in the Christian life but you're not sure how to make them a part of your prayers.

Take heart! This book was written just for you. I can promise you that if you follow it faithfully that the Lord will change you and change the world through your prayers! How can I make such a promise? Because this book is based solely upon the Scriptures and God promises that *His* Words will *never* come back empty! "My Word will not return to me empty, but will accomplish what I desire and achieve the purpose for which I sent it." (Isa. 55:11) When you live and pray according to His will as made known by His Words in the Bible, He promises to answer you!

This book is a non-denominational, practical, easy to use, scripturally based means by which you can obey God's will for prayer. He commands each and every Christian to be devoted to prayer (Col. 4:2), to pray for all the saints at all times with all kinds of prayers and requests (Eph. 6:18), to pray for all those in authority so the lost will be saved (1 Tim. 2:1-4), to pray for the nations of the world to belong to Christ (Psa. 2:8), to confess our sins (1 John 1:9), to praise Him continually (Heb. 13:15), to be faithful in prayer (Rom. 12:12), and to pray continuously (1 Th. 5:17). By using this book, you will be able to obey these commands and have a clear conscience before God!

In addition, because you will be praying in the Word of God, you will have the right to claim this promise for answered prayer, "If you remain in Me and My words remain in you, ask whatever you wish, and it will be given to you." And by confessing your sins regularly and submitting yourself to God's will, you will have confidence to claim another promise of answered prayer, "Dear friends, if our hearts do not condemn us we have confidence before God and receive from Him anything we ask, because we obey His commands and do what pleases Him."

My husband, Paul, and I have spoken to nineteen different denominations in nineteen states about prayer and been received by thousands of Christians with joy! Time and time again, we have heard from people just like you who have longed for a deeper and more fulfilling prayer life that using this book has revolutionized their intimacy with God and their sense of partnership with Him in accomplishing His purposes.

Let's take this prayer journey together! You can know for certain that each time you use this book that I will be there with you in spirit saying "yes!" to each prayer that you pray. Together we will be Christ's prayer partners for the advancement of His Kingdom.

> With His love,
> Kathie Grant

FOREWORD

In 1975, Moody Press published my first book, *The Adversary*. In 1984, its sequel, *Overcoming the Adversary*, came into print. Both of these books carry the message of seeking to help Christian people know the importance of incorporating doctrinal truth into their practice of prayer. Each book contains a number of written prayers that provide examples of including Biblical doctrine in prayer. The Lord had graciously taught me that doctrinal truth is not just something one learns in church or in Bible college. God's Truth is something He intends for His people to apply and live out in every life situation.

In 1996, it was my privilege to get to know Paul and Kathie Grant during a time of prayer and spiritual encouragement. As a gesture of appreciation for the time we spent together, Kathie gave me two copies of a developing work on prayer the Lord had put on her heart. Later, as I had time to examine the material, emotions of excitement began to stir within me. I saw Kathie's work as a tool that really could teach people to incorporate God's Word into their practice of prayer. I remember calling them and urging them to work toward putting the notebook into a published format that would help people to learn doctrinal prayer. This book is the fruit of their work.

Kathie Grant stated in a letter to me, "It was your book, *The Adversary* that taught me to pray and to claim my position in Christ during the early months of my salvation." I am deeply honored by her testimony, but it is even a greater honor that she took the truth I sought to convey and developed a teaching and learning tool for God's people. As people learn "praying in the Word of God" we will indeed see Christ's Kingdom advancing! I believe the kind of prayer this book helps Christian's develop to be an integral part to our Lord bringing revival to these troubled times. It is God's Truth that defeats evil and moves God to honor the might and power of His Word.

One of the spiritual milestones in my own prayer life has been the memorizing of many of the Bible's prayer Psalms. During my morning walks,

I've learned to pray these memorized Psalms back to God. This has always proved to be refreshing and spiritually invigorating. God keeps using these divinely inspired prayers to teach me a deeper level of intimacy with Him and trust in His promises.

Praying in the Word of God will bring that same kind of spiritual refreshing into the life of each Christian who follows its provided guidance. It will help you to learn to pray God's Word back to Him. I believe this book to be one of the very best on the subject of prayer! I urgently commend it to all who want the Lord Jesus Christ to "teach us to pray"!

Dr. Mark I. Bubeck, acting President and President Emeritus
The International Center for Biblical Counseling
1551 Indian Hills Drive, Suite 200
Sioux City, IA 51104

CONTENTS

PRAYING FOR BELIEVERS

PRAYING FOR THE LOST

CONCLUSION

PRAYER PARTNERS WITH GOD

This is the confidence we have in approaching God:
that if we ask anything according to His will,
He hears us.
And if we know that He hears us – whatever we ask –
we know that we have what we asked of Him.
1 John 5:14-15

As You Begin

Most books on prayer are about the theory of prayer. This book is different because you *use* it as you pray! Organized solely upon the Scriptures, it guides you to pray systematically and comprehensively for the advancement of God's Kingdom in your life and in the world. In just 15 to 20 minutes a day, you will be led by the Lord through His Words in praise, confession, petition, and intercession. You will be enabled to pray faithfully for yourself, your loved ones, other believers, your church, missionaries, the lost, and all the nations of the world.

This daily prayer book also includes pages on which to journal your personal praise to God, to record personal prayers and answers to prayer, and to list the names of believers and unbelievers. It provides an opportunity to be convicted of sin by reading and submitting to the commandments of God and a place to journal your own personal confession of sin. In addition, it teaches you how to intercede for the sins of your loved ones, for the Church at Large, and for your local fellowship, enabling you to participate in your role as a priest on behalf of the Body of Christ.

To continue our mission to advance Christ's Kingdom in the world, it provides maps of all the nations of the world plus graphs that tell their main religious affiliations. A list is also provided of all the Christian denominations in America of five thousand or more. These unique elements give you the opportunity to pray for the renewal of Christians in America and around the world, the salvation of the lost worldwide, and for persecuted believers in fifty-seven nations.

Praying for His Kingdom

The purpose of this book is to enable you to partner with our Lord in establishing His Kingdom on earth as it is in heaven as the Lord's prayer commands us to do, "Thy Kingdom come, Thy will be done." Christ came to establish a Kingdom on earth of those people, who by His grace, would desire and be able to obey His commands. His Kingdom exists in each of us individually when we trust in Him as Savior and Lord, and in the Church as a whole as we walk together in that same loving and faithful obedience.

When we make His Kingdom the purpose of our lives and live to please Him, the Scripture promises that we can ask God in prayer to accomplish

His Kingdom purposes and He will do it! One of the most wonderful promises for answered prayer is 1 John 5:14-15: "Dear friends, if our hearts do not condemn us, we have confidence before God and receive from Him anything we ask, because we obey His commands and do what pleases Him." Notice that this verse promises that we can ask "*anything*" if we are living to please God and obeying his commands! This book will enable the "anything" you ask for to be His glory and His Kingdom.

Two other promises of answered prayer will give you the same confidence that when you live to seek His Kingdom that God will give you whatever you ask are: "Until now you have not asked for anything in My name. Ask and you will receive and your joy will be complete." (John 16:24) "And I will do whatever you ask for in My name, so the Son may bring glory to the Father. You may ask Me for anything in My name, and I will do it." (John 14: 13-14) This book will enable you to focus your prayers upon the purpose of your life enabling you to satisfy this condition for answered prayer.

PRAYING IN THE WORD OF GOD

The reason this book is based upon the Word of God is that the Word does the following: sets us apart from sin (John 17:17), is living and active, penetrates to dividing the soul and the spirit, and judges the thoughts and attitudes of the heart (Heb. 4:12), is God-breathed and useful for teaching, rebuking, correcting and training in righteousness (2 Tim. 3:16), will never pass away (Matt. 24:35), never returns empty (Isa. 55:11), and is authored by the Holy Spirit (2 Pe. 1:21). The Scriptures are inerrant and infallible, the only dependable guide for all of life and godliness—and that includes one's prayer life.

From the beginning to the end of the Bible, God testifies to the primacy of prayer in the life of His people and how He is the God who both inspires and answers prayer.

The Scriptures reveal His will, purposes, and plans and how prayer accomplishes both.

1 John 5:14-15 promises us that when we find God's will in the Scripture that we can ask Him to accomplish it and He will: "This is the confidence in approaching God: that if we ask anything according to His will, He hears us. And if we know that He hears us—whatever we ask—we

know that we have what we asked of Him." This book will enable you to know for certain what God's will is and give you confidence to pray for it to be done.

The Scriptures also reveal God's commands, conditions, and promises concerning prayer. John 15:7 specifically connects Christ's Words remaining in us with answered prayer: "If you remain in Me and My words remain in you, ask whatever you wish, and it will be given to you." This book will enable you to meet this condition for answered prayer. As you pray in the Word of God, He will transform your heart and mind, enabling you to become a person with a heart like His whose prayers are answered.

Another condition for answered prayer is faith. Jesus said, "If you believe, you will receive whatever you ask for in prayer." (Matt. 21:22) Romans 10:17 reveals that faith is formed in us through the Word of God, "Consequently, faith comes from hearing the message, and the message is heard through the Word of Christ." As you pray in the Word of God, the Holy Spirit will cause faith in His Words to grow in your heart and mind enabling you to meet this condition of answered prayer.

The Scriptures also say that only the prayers of the righteous are heard, "The Lord is far from the wicked but he hears the prayer of the righteous." (Pro. 15:29) "We know that God does not listen to sinners. He listens to the godly man who does His will." (John 9:31) It is the Word, through the ministry of the Holy Spirit, which sets us apart from sin so that we might walk in righteousness in order to fulfill this condition for answered prayer. Jesus prayed, "Sanctify them by the truth; your Word is truth." The author of Hebrews tells us what the Word does to sanctify us from sin: "For the Word of God is living and active. Sharper than any double-edged sword, it penetrates to dividing soul and spirit, joints and marrow; it judges the thoughts and attitudes of the heart." (Heb. 4:12)

As you use this book in prayer, you will discover that the Word of God is living and active in your life, separating you from sin and enabling you to walk in righteousness and to claim His promises to the righteous concerning answered prayer.

HOW USING THIS BOOK CAN AFFECT YOUR LIFE

You will be brought closer to the Lord Jesus Christ as your mind is renewed through Scriptural prayers by His Word and as you become His prayer partner in praying for the Church and for the lost. The focus of your prayers will shift from yourself to God, from your needs to His will, from your glory to His glory, from the narrow circle of your family and friends to His Church and the world He wants to impact with the gospel. You will develop confidence in prayer and your faith will grow as your prayers are answered. You will be enabled to pray faithfully for yourself, your loved ones, other believers, your church, the lost, missionaries, our nation, and all the nations of the world. You will discover that, although you may never be a missionary to another nation, you are a missionary in prayer for the whole world.

There is no greater ministry than prayer! There is no greater means given to us from God than prayer to impact this world for Christ! You may speak to a thousand people in your lifetime but you can pray for millions.

It is entirely possible that you will stand one day before the Lord, our precious Savior, and hear Him say, "Turn around. See what your prayers have accomplished! Well done my good and faithful servant!" And behind you will be thousands and thousands of people, perhaps millions, out of every tribe, language, people, and nation, who are in the Kingdom of God because you prayed.

PRACTICAL ENCOURAGEMENT

Only the Bible is inerrant and infallible! You need not agree with every application of every verse to use this book. Feel free to disregard whatever conflicts with your personal belief. Use this book according to your conscience and the leading of the Holy Spirit. It is my sincerest hope and prayer that you will make this book work for you as you seek to live for Him. While this book was written with the sincerest of intentions— to glorify Christ, to be faithful to His Words and to His will, and to advance His Kingdom—it is only useful if you make it your own. So "edit" it for your best use!

In terms of how to use it in your life, I would encourage you to be gentle with yourself! If you are not used to praying for more than a few minutes at a time, don't try to use it at first for longer than about fifteen minutes. If you go longer than that, you may become discouraged and not use it again. So set your timer and end after fifteen minutes! Forming a habit of daily prayer often takes years. Do not become discouraged! If you will persist, even if you fail for a long time, you will eventually succeed.

You are the only one who can decide when to use the book. It is clear from the Scripture and our own experience, that praying first thing in the morning is probably best. I certainly recommend it because " His mercies are new every morning" and because we all know how difficult it is to pray a session of prayer once the busyness of the day takes over. Yet some of you are simply unable to pray in the morning. Pick another time and make it a priority; God is awake twenty-four hours a day!

While using it everyday is best, certainly this is a book that can be used in many other ways—several times a week, once a week, for a two hour session once a month, etc.

While it was written primarily for use in personal devotions, it is also works well in praying with your spouse, with older children, in a small group, in a Bible study, in mid-week prayer meetings, and during Sunday morning services. It is for all ages from 16 on up, men and women, lay people, pastors, teachers, missionaries, leaders in the church, brand new Christians and mature believers, and Christians of all denominations who believe in the Word of God.

May this book revolutionize your prayer life, drawing you closer to the Lord Jesus Christ and enabling you to become His prayer partner for His Kingdom's sake!

Dear friends, if our hearts do not condemn us,
we have confidence before God and receive from Him
anything we ask, because we obey His commands
and do what pleases Him.
1 John 3:21-22

How to Use This Book in a Session of Prayer

This book is a buffet of God's Words as they reveal His will and purposes for prayer. Just as you wouldn't eat all the appetizers, main dishes and desserts at a Sunday buffet, don't feel you must pray every prayer every time you have a session of prayer.

As you use this book to come to God in prayer each day, read only one or two verse/prayer sets from each chapter of the book, focusing on the presence of God and adding your faith and love to each one. Remember to come to God and expect to hear from Him! Read as few or as many prayer/verse sets as you choose. In longer prayers, read just a paragraph or part of a paragraph. Please feel free to pray your own prayer back to God as the Holy Spirit leads you. But do not feel that you must come up with your own prayer. When you add your affirmation by faith and love to the prayers in this book, God accepts them as your own.

There are four sections in the book with several chapters within each for a total of twenty-seven chapters:

1. *Praise* – for who God is, for the inheritance He has given us in Christ, and for all the personal ways He is at work in your life

2. *Confession of Sin* – personal confession, intercession for your family, for the Church at large, and for your local church

3. *Praying for Believers* – New Testament prayers for believers, prayers asking God to accomplish His will in the life of believers, prayers for revival of Christian denominations, a place to list the names of believers, prayers for persecuted believers in fifty-seven nations, personal prayer requests, and a place to record answers to prayer

4. *Prayers for the Lost* – God's will for the lost, salvation verses and prayers for the lost, a place to list the names of the lost, prayers for our nation, prayers for all the nations of the world, maps and lists of all the nations including graphs that tell their main religious affiliations

To use this book during a time of prayer, start by turning to the Praise Section. It begins with verses from the Bible that reveal the attributes of

God. Each verse is followed by a prayer praising God for the attributes mentioned in the verse. Read the verse and prayer aloud or to yourself as a praise to God combining them with your faith and love. You may re-phrase the prayer response to the verse in your own words or make it a starting point for your own prayer to God.

You may read as many or as few verse/prayer sets from the Praise Section each day as you choose. Next, go on to the other sections and do the same. You may find it helpful to mark the twenty-seven chapters with tabs from an office supply store. In addition, you may choose to use Post-It notes to mark where you stop within each chapter. This way you will know where to begin the next time you have a session of prayer. If you pray one verse/prayer set each day from each of the twenty-seven chapters, it will take you only fifteen to twenty minutes to go through the book!

The purpose of this book is to help you to become more complete, systematic, and faithful in your prayer life as you are led by our Lord through His Words. Jesus said, "Heaven and earth will pass away, but My words will never pass away." Relying on the Word of God to lead and guide you in prayer is always fruitful for His Words never return empty.

PRAISE

*Praise the Lord. Praise God in His sanctuary; praise Him
in His mighty heavens. Praise Him for His acts of power;
praise Him for His surpassing greatness.
Let everything that has breath praise the Lord.
Praise the Lord.
Psalm 150:1,2,6*

PRAISE

This is the most important prayer section. Without a proper acknowledgment of who God is and why He deserves and therefore demands our complete obedience and consecration, no other prayer can follow. God only hears and answers the prayers of His consecrated saints, who live to do His will by faith in Christ Jesus, the Lord.

There are five chapters on praising God:

1. *Praising God for Who He Is* – Verses from the Bible that reveal God's attributes, followed by prayers that pray these Scriptures back to God.
2. *An Overview of Verses That Reveal Our New Identity and Inheritance in Christ* – Verses that give an overview of our wealth "in Christ," to be used in praising God.
3. *Praising God for Our New Identity and Inheritance in Christ* – Eighty-eight verses that praise God for all He gave us when He gave us His Son, each followed by a prayer expressing thanks to God for the gifts mentioned in the verses.
4. *Praising God for Who I Am in Christ* – Seventy-two verses that reveal our identity "in Christ," to be used in praise.
5. *Personal Praise and Thanksgiving* – a place to thank and praise God for what He is doing in your life, family, church and in the Body of Christ as a whole.

HOW TO USE THE PRAISE SECTION

Starting with *Praising God for Who He Is*, read the verses and prayers aloud or to yourself, focusing on the presence of God and adding your faith and love to each verse. Remember to come to God! Read as few or as many verses each day as you choose, marking where you leave off with a paper clip. The prayers following the verses have been included in order to teach you how to pray Scripture back to God. Therefore, please feel free to pray your own prayer back to God as the Holy Spirit leads you. But do not feel that you have to come up with your own prayer. When you add your affirmation by faith and in love to both the verses and the prayers, your heart is worshiping God and He receives them as your own.

The next chapter is *An Overview of Verses That Reveal Our New Identity and Inheritance in Christ*. These verses give a picture of the wealth we have in Christ. Use them in the same way—reading them to God as your prayer of love, faith and affirmation.

Each day, continue on with *Praising God for Our New Identity and Inheritance in Christ*. This chapter is set up like the first chapter: Verses followed by prayers. Read these aloud to God, making them your own prayer of praise.

The fourth chapter is a list of many of the attributes of our new identity in Christ. Read these to God, thanking Him for who you are because of Christ Jesus, your Savior and Lord.

The final chapter in the Praise section is your personal thanks and praise to God.

Praising God for Who He Is

O Lord, You are my God; I will exalt You and praise Your name, for in perfect faithfulness You have done marvelous things, things planned long ago…"Surely this is our God; we trusted in Him, and He saved us. This is the Lord, we trusted in Him; let us rejoice and be glad in His salvation." (Isa. 25:1,9)

> Dearest heavenly Father,
>
> We exalt You as our God and praise Your holy name for all the marvelous things that You have done. You are our God and the God of all who have trusted in You, whom You have saved. We rejoice in our salvation, and we are filled with gladness!
>
> Because of Christ Jesus, Amen

"Worthy is the Lamb, who was slain, to receive power and wealth and wisdom and strength and honor and glory and praise!" (Rev. 5:12)

> Dearest Lord Jesus,
>
> Worthy are You, the Lamb of God, because You were slain for our sins and for the sins of the whole world. We desire that You receive all power and wealth and wisdom and strength and honor and glory and praise! Thank You for Your blood, which was shed for the forgiveness of our sins.
>
> With all my devotion, Amen

"You are worthy, our Lord and God, to receive glory and honor and power, for You created all things, and by Your will they were created and have their being." (Rev. 4:11)

> Dear heavenly Father,
>
> You are worthy to receive our honor — and all honor, glory and power because You have created all things by Your will. We acknowledge You and worship You as our Creator and as the creator of all things. And we give You our lives as living sacrifices, today and every day, to do Your will for Your glory.
>
> For the glory of my Creator, Amen

But about the Son he says, "Your throne, O God, will last for ever and ever, and righteousness will be the scepter of Your kingdom. You have loved righteousness and hated wickedness; therefore God, Your God, has set You above Your companions by anointing You with the oil of joy." (Heb. 1:8,9)

Dear heavenly Father,

We worship Your Son in His majesty on the throne at Your right hand, and we rejoice with You over Him and the eternal kingdom He has brought within each of us who believe and will bring to this earth when He returns – a kingdom of righteousness. Thank You, dearest LORD Jesus, for loving righteousness and hating wickedness. Thank You, Father, for setting Your Son above all and anointing Him with the oil of joy!

In Christ, Amen

In the beginning was the Word, and the Word was with God, and the Word was God. He was with God in the beginning. The Word became flesh and made His dwelling among us...No one has ever seen God, but God the One and Only, who is at the Father's side, has made Him known. "For God so loved the world that He gave His one and only Son, that whoever believes in Him shall not perish but have eternal life." (John 1:1,2,14,18, 3:16)

Dearest Lord Jesus,

You are eternally God! No one but You has ever seen God but You have made Him known. You became a man and lived among us to save us. We worship You as Savior and Lord.

Amen

The Son is the radiance of God's glory and the exact representation of His being, sustaining all things by His powerful word. After He had provided purification for sins, He sat down at the right hand of the Majesty in heaven. (Heb. 1:3)

Dearest Lord Jesus,

We worship You as the very radiance of God's glory and the exact

5

representation of the being of the Father. We worship You as the One who sustains all things in the universe by Your powerful Word. We affirm with awe and adoration that after You provided purification for our sins and for the sins of the whole world, You sat down at the right hand of the Father in heaven.

You are almighty God! Amen

Now to Him who is able to establish you by my gospel and the proclamation of Jesus Christ, according to the revelation of the mystery hidden for long ages past, but now revealed and made known through the prophetic writings by the command of the eternal God, so that all nations might believe and obey Him — to the only wise God be glory forever through Jesus Christ! Amen (Rom. 16:27)

Dear heavenly Father,

We give You glory as the only wise God, who is able to establish Your church by the gospel and proclamation of the Lord Jesus Christ! We thank You and praise You that the gospel is no longer a mystery, but has been revealed through the Bible by the Holy Spirit to us who believe. We thank You that this glorious gospel, salvation by faith in Christ, is for all the nations of the world. We pray that out of all nations the gospel will draw many to believe and obey You through Jesus Christ, our Lord. Amen

He saved us through the washing of rebirth and renewal by the Holy Spirit, whom He poured out on us generously through Jesus Christ our Savior..., Yet to all who received Him, to those who believed in His name, He gave the right to become children of God— children born not of natural descent, nor of human decision or a husband's will, but born of God. (Titus 3:5b,6, John 1:12-13)

Dear heavenly Father,

Thank You for pouring out on us the Holy Spirit through whom You have given us rebirth and renewal enabling us to believe in Jesus Christ as Savior, to receive Him and to become Your children.

With gratitude and thanksgiving, Amen

He is the image of the invisible God, the firstborn over all creation. For by Him all things were created: things in heaven and on earth, visible and invisible, whether thrones or powers or rulers or authorities; all things were created by Him and for Him. He is before all things, and in Him all things hold together. (Col. 1:15-17)

> Dearest Lord Jesus Christ,
>
> In You we see who God is! You are the firstborn over all creation, and it is through You and for You that all things were created. Not only this, but You are before all things, and in You all things hold together. We praise You for who You are: the author and sustainer of all creation. Amen

Oh, the depth of the riches of the wisdom and knowledge of God! How unsearchable His judgments, and His paths beyond tracing out! "Who has known the mind of the Lord? Or who has been His counselor?" "Who has ever given to God, that God should repay Him?" For from Him and through Him and to Him are all things. To Him be the glory forever! Amen (Rom. 11:33-36)

> Dearest Father,
>
> Who indeed has ever given to You, that You should repay him? Surely none of us know the depths of the riches of Your wisdom, knowledge, judgments, or paths! We are not worthy to be Your counselors. We acknowledge that it is from You and through You and to You that all things are. We ascribe to You glory!
>
> In the radiance of Your glory, Christ Jesus, Amen

And I will ask the Father, and He will give you another Counselor to be with you forever — the Spirit of truth…when He, the Spirit of truth, comes, He will guide you into all truth…the Counselor, the Holy Spirit, whom the Father will send in My name, will teach you all things and will remind you of everything I have said to you. (John 14:16-17, 16:13-14, 14:26)

> Dearest Lord Jesus
>
> Thank You for giving us the Holy Spirit to counsel us, to be unto us the Spirit of truth who guides us into all the truth, who teaches

us all things, and who reminds us of everything You have said.

With thanksgiving, Amen

Having believed, you were marked in Him with a seal, the promised Holy Spirit, who is a deposit guaranteeing our inheritance until the redemption of those who are God's possession — to the praise of His glory. And we, who with unveiled faces all reflect the Lord's glory, are being transformed into His likeness with ever-increasing glory, which comes from the Lord, who is the Spirit. (Eph. 1:13-14, 2 Cor. 3:18)

Dearest Holy Spirit,

Thank You for marking us as God's possession. Your presence in us guarantees our redemption and is for the praise of the glory of God. Thank You also for Your blessed ministry in our lives whereby You cause us to be transformed into the likeness of our dearest Lord Jesus as we reflect His glory. Thank You, Blessed Holy Spirit, that You are one with the Lord Jesus Christ and wherever You are so is He.

With thanksgiving, Amen

"To Him who sits on the throne and to the Lamb be praise and honor and glory and power, for ever and ever!" (Rev. 5:13)

Dearest almighty Father and Son,

To You who sit on the throne, our heavenly Father, and to the Son, the Lamb of God slain for our sins, we ascribe praise, honor, glory and power—forever and ever!

From hearts full of love, Amen

O LORD, our LORD, how majestic is Your name in all the earth! You have set Your glory above the heavens. When I consider Your heavens, the work of Your fingers, the moon and the stars, which You have set in place, what is man that You are mindful of him, the son of man that You care for him? (Psa. 8:1,3,4)

Oh, Lord Jesus,

We marvel at the glory of the heavens, which are the work of Your fingers—of the moon and stars, which You set in place. We wonder with humility how it is that You have been mindful of us! How could You possibly care for us? How majestic is Your name in all the earth!

With thanksgiving, Amen

I will praise You, O LORD, with all my heart; I will tell of all Your wonders. I will be glad and rejoice in You; I will sing praise to Your name, O Most High. (Psa. 9:1,2)

Dear Father in heaven,

We will praise You with all our hearts; we will tell of all Your wonders. We will be glad and rejoice in You and sing praises to Your name,

O Most High God. Amen

The Lord reigns forever; He has established His throne for judgment. He will judge the world in righteousness; He will govern the peoples with justice. (Psa. 9:7,8)

Dear Lord Jesus,

You have established Your throne for judgment and will judge the world in righteousness and govern all peoples with justice. We long for the day when You will establish Your kingdom on this earth and we will rule and reign over all nations with You.

For Your glory, Amen

Sing praises to the LORD, enthroned in Zion; proclaim among the nations what He has done. For He who avenges blood remembers; He does not ignore the cry of the afflicted. (Psa. 9:11,12)

Dear LORD,

We praise You, O King, enthroned in Zion, for You will avenge the blood of Your saints and will answer the cry of the afflicted! Enable the proclamation of the glory of Christ to go forth among all the nations for all that He has done and will do! And encourage us

who are under affliction to wait upon Him who does not ignore
our cry.

> In the name of the One who hears, Amen

I love You, O LORD, my strength. The Lord is my rock, my fortress and my
deliverer; my God is my rock, in whom I take refuge. He is my shield and
the horn of my salvation, my stronghold. I call to the Lord, who is worthy of
praise, and I am saved from my enemies. (Psa. 18:1–3)

> Dearest Lord Jesus,
>
> You are my rock, my fortress, and my deliverer, and I take refuge
> in You today. Be my shield, the horn of my salvation and my
> stronghold. I call to You, the One who is worthy of praise, and **am**
> saved from my enemies! I praise You for Your deliverance.
>
> In the name of my deliverer, the Lord Jesus, Amen

Lift up your heads, O you gates; be lifted up, you ancient doors, that the
King of glory may come in. Who is this King of glory? The LORD strong and
mighty, the Lord mighty in battle. Lift up your heads, O you gates; lift them
up, you ancient doors, that the King of glory may come in. Who is He, this
King of glory? The LORD Almighty — He is the King of glory. *Selah* (Psa.
24:7-10)

> Dear King of glory, the Lord Jesus Christ,
>
> We worship You as the King of glory and magnify Your name, for
> You are strong and mighty. You are, indeed, the almighty LORD.
> You have overcome all the enemies of our souls. We lift up our
> heads and open the doors of our hearts to give You glory and ask
> that You rule and reign in us, both now and forevermore.
>
> In the King of glory, Amen

The LORD is my light and my salvation — whom shall I fear? The LORD is
the stronghold of my life — of whom shall I be afraid? One thing I ask of
the Lord, this is what I seek: that I may dwell in the house of the Lord all
the days of my life, to gaze upon the beauty of the LORD and to seek Him in
His temple. For in the day of trouble He will keep me safe in His dwelling;
He will hide me in the shelter of His tabernacle and set me high upon a
rock. Then my head will be exalted above the enemies who surround me;

at His tabernacle will I sacrifice with shouts of joy; I will sing and make
music to the Lord. (Psa. 27:1,4-6)

> Dearest Lord Jesus,
>
> You are my light and salvation; help me not to fear! You are the
> stronghold I run to; help me not to be afraid! Truly, my LORD and
> God, I ask of You and seek with all my heart to find my hiding
> place in You, where You will keep me safe and shelter me, setting
> me high upon the rock that is You. I shout to You with joy; I will
> sing and make music to You, for You have exalted me above all the
> enemies of my soul!
>
> > With rejoicing, Amen

Praise the Lord. Praise, O servants of the LORD, praise the name of the
LORD. Let the name of the LORD be praised, both now and forevermore.
From the rising of the sun to the place where it sets, the name of the Lord
is to be praised. The LORD is exalted over all the nations, His glory above
the heavens. Who is like the LORD our God, The One who sits enthroned
on high, who stoops down to look on the heavens and the earth? He raises
the poor from the dust and lifts the needy from the ash heap; He seats them
with princes, with the princes of their people. He settles the barren woman
in her home as a happy mother of children. Praise the Lord. (Psa. 113)

> Dear heavenly Father,
>
> Truly we praise You and exalt Your name forever! You are exalted
> over all the nations, and Your glory is above the heavens. Who is
> like You, our Lord and God, who sits enthroned on high, who stoops
> down to look on the heavens and the earth? You raise the poor
> from the dust and lift the needy from poverty and seat them with
> leaders. You have mercy on the barren woman and give her a happy
> home as the mother of her own children. Praise the LORD!
>
> > For the glory of God, Amen

"Give thanks to the LORD, call on His name; make known among the na-
tions what He has done, and proclaim that His name is exalted. Sing to the
Lord, for He has done glorious things; let this be known to all the world.
Shout aloud and sing for joy, people of Zion, for great is the Holy One of
Israel among you." (Isa. 12:4-6)

Dear LORD,

We sing to You for You have done a glorious thing! You have given us salvation through Your Son. We long that Your salvation by faith in Christ Jesus be made known all over the world! Great are You, the Holy One of Israel, for Your salvation! We shout and sing to You for joy!

With love and thanksgiving, Amen

℘

Please continue with the following verses, saying them to God as the praise of your heart, then restating them, if you choose, in your own prayer to God.

I saw heaven standing open and there before me was a white horse, whose rider is called Faithful and True. With justice He judges and makes war. His eyes are like blazing fire, and on His head are many crowns. He has a name written on Him that no one knows but He Himself. He is dressed in a robe dipped in blood, and His name is the Word of God. On His robe and on His thigh He has this name written: KING OF KINGS AND LORD OF LORDS. (Rev. 19:11-13,16)

Then I heard what sounded like a great multitude, like the roar of rushing waters and like loud peals of thunder, shouting: "Hallelujah! For our Lord God Almighty reigns. Let us rejoice and be glad and give Him glory! For the wedding of the Lamb has come, and His bride has made herself ready. Fine linen, bright and clean, was given her to wear." (Fine linen stands for the righteous acts of the saints.) (Rev. 19:6-8)

"Here is My servant, whom I uphold, My chosen one in whom I delight; I will put My Spirit on Him and He will bring justice to the nations. He will not shout or cry out, or raise His voice in the streets. A bruised reed He will not break, and a smoldering wick He will not snuff out. In faithfulness He will bring forth justice; He will not falter or be discouraged till He establishes justice on earth. In His law the islands will put their hope." (Isa. 42:1-4)

This is what God the LORD says — He who created the heavens and stretched them out, who spread out the earth and all that comes out of it, who gives breath to its people, and life to those who walk on it: "I, the LORD, have called you in righteousness; I will take hold of your hand. I will keep you and will make you to be a covenant for the people and a light for the Gentiles, to open eyes that are blind, to free captives from prison and to release from the dungeon those who sit in darkness." (Isa. 42:5-7)

I lift up my eyes to the hills — where does my help come from? My help comes from the LORD, the Maker of heaven and earth. He will not let your foot slip — He who watches over you will not slumber; indeed, He who watches over Israel will neither slumber nor sleep. The LORD watches over you — the LORD is your shade at your right hand; the sun will not harm you by day, nor the moon by night. The LORD will keep you from all harm — He will watch over your life; the Lord will watch over your coming and going both now and forevermore. (Psa. 121:1-8)

Praise the LORD. Praise the LORD from the heavens, praise Him in the heights above. Praise Him, all His angels, praise Him, all His heavenly hosts. Praise Him, sun and moon, praise Him, all you shining stars. Praise Him, you highest heavens and you waters above the skies. Let them praise the name of the LORD, for He commanded and they were created. He set them in place for ever and ever; He gave a decree that will never pass away. (Psa. 148:1-6)

Before the mountains were born or You brought forth the earth and the world, from everlasting to everlasting You are God. You turn men back to dust, saying, "Return to dust, O sons of men." For a thousand years in Your sight are like a day that has just gone by, or like a watch in the night. (Psa. 90:2-4)

The LORD reigns, He is robed in majesty; the Lord is robed in majesty and is armed with strength. The world is firmly established; it cannot be moved. Your throne was established long ago; You are from all eternity. The seas have lifted up, O LORD, the seas have lifted up their voice; the seas have lifted up their pounding waves. Mightier than the thunder of the great waters, mightier than the breakers of the sea – the LORD on high is mighty. (Psa. 93:1-4)

But the LORD is the true God; He is the living God, the eternal King. When He is angry, the earth trembles; the nations cannot endure His wrath. "Tell them this: 'These gods, who did not make the heavens and the earth, will perish from the earth and from under the heavens.'" But God made the earth by His power; He founded the world by His wisdom and stretched out the heavens by His understanding. When He thunders, the waters in the heavens roar; He makes clouds rise from the ends of the earth. He sends lightning with the rain and brings out the wind from His storehouses. (Jer. 10:10-13)

In the beginning You laid the foundations of the earth, and the heavens are the work of Your hands. They will perish, but You remain; they will all wear out like a garment. Like clothing You will change them and they will be discarded. But You remain the same, and Your years will never end. (Psa. 102:25-27)

For My own name's sake I delay My wrath; for the sake of My praise I hold it back from you, so as not to cut you off. See, I have refined you, though not as silver; I have tested you in the furnace of affliction. For My own sake, for My own sake, I do this. How can I let myself be defamed? I will not yield My glory to another. "Listen to Me, O Jacob, Israel, whom I have called: I am He; I am the first and I am the last. My own hand laid the foundations of the earth, and My right hand spread out the heavens; when I summon them, they all stand up together. (Isa. 48:9-13)

God said to Moses, "I AM WHO I AM." (Ex. 3:14)

Then Moses said, "Now show me Your glory." And the LORD said, "I will cause all My goodness to pass in front of you, and I will proclaim My name, the LORD, in your presence. I will have mercy on whom I will have mercy, and I will have compassion on whom I will have compassion. But," He said, "you cannot see My face, for no one may see Me and live." (Ex. 33:18-20)

Every good and perfect gift is from above, coming down from the Father of the heavenly lights, who does not change like shifting shadows. (James 1:17)

A voice says, "Cry out." And I said, "What shall I cry?" "All men are like grass, and all their glory is like the flowers of the field. The grass withers and the flowers fall, because the breath of the Lord blows on them. Surely the people are grass. The grass withers and the flowers fall, but the word of our God stands forever." (Isa. 40:6-8)

Your word, O Lord, is eternal; it stands firm in the heavens...Yet You are near, O Lord, and all Your commands are true. Long ago I learned from Your statutes that You established them to last forever...and the Scripture cannot be broken...(Psa. 119:89,151,152; John 10:35)

He who is the Glory of Israel does not lie or change His mind; for He is not a man, that He should change His mind."...God is not a man, that He should lie, nor a son of man, that He should change His mind. Does He speak and then not act? Does He promise and not fulfill? (1 Sam. 15:29; Num. 23:19)

But the plans of the Lord stand firm forever, the purposes of His heart through all generations...God wanted to make the unchanging nature of His purpose very clear...(Psa. 33:11; Heb. 6:17)

Jesus Christ is the same yesterday and today and forever...Therefore He is able to save completely those who come to God through Him, because He always lives to intercede for them. (Heb. 13:8; 7:25)

The Lord is gracious and compassionate, slow to anger and rich in love. The Lord is good to all; He has compassion on all He has made. All You have made will praise You, O Lord; Your saints will extol You. They will tell of the glory of Your kingdom and speak of Your might, so that all men may know of Your mighty acts and the glorious splendor of Your kingdom. Your kingdom is an everlasting kingdom, and Your dominion endures through all generations. The Lord is faithful to all His promises and loving toward all He has made. (Psa. 145:8-13)

Let us come before Him with thanksgiving and extol Him with music and song. For the Lord is the great God, the great King above all gods. In His hand are the depths of the earth, and the mountain peaks belong to Him. The sea is His, for He made it, and His hands formed the dry land. Come, let us bow down in worship, let us kneel before the Lord our maker; for He is our God and we are the people of His pasture, the flock under His care...(Psa. 95:2-7)

Is anything too hard for the LORD?..."Ah, Sovereign LORD, You have made the heavens and the earth by Your great power and outstretched arm. Nothing is too hard for You..." I am the LORD, the God of all mankind. Is anything too hard for Me? (Gen. 18:14; Jer. 32:17,27)

O LORD, You have searched me and You know me. You know when I sit and when I rise; You perceive my thoughts from afar. You discern my going out and my lying down; You are familiar with all my ways. Before a word is on my tongue You know it completely, O LORD. You hem me in — behind and before; You have laid Your hand upon me. Such knowledge is too wonderful for me, too lofty for me to attain. Where can I go from Your Spirit? Where can I flee from Your presence?...For You created my inmost being; You knit me together in my mother's womb. (Psa. 139:1-7,13)

Out of the north He comes in golden splendor; God comes in awesome majesty. The Almighty is beyond our reach and exalted in power; in His justice and great righteousness, He does not oppress. (Job 37:22,23)

Then the LORD spoke to Job out of the storm: "Brace yourself like a man; I will question you, and you shall answer Me. Would you discredit My justice? Would you condemn Me to justify yourself? Do you have an arm like God's, and can your voice thunder like His? Then adorn yourself with glory and splendor, and clothe yourself in honor and majesty. Unleash the fury of your wrath, look at every proud man and bring him low, look at every proud man and humble him, crush the wicked where they stand. Bury them all in the dust together; shroud their faces in the grave. Then I myself will admit to you that your own right hand can save you." (Job 40:6-14)

Who has measured the waters in the hollow of His hand, or with the breadth of His hand marked off the heavens? Who has held the dust of the earth in a basket, or weighed the mountains on the scales and the hills in a balance? Who has understood the mind of the LORD, or instructed Him as His counselor? Whom did the Lord consult to enlighten Him, and who taught Him the right way? Who was it that taught Him knowledge or showed Him the path of understanding? (Isa. 40:12-14)

His wisdom is profound, His power is vast. Who has resisted Him and come out unscathed?…"To God belong wisdom and power; counsel and understanding are His…" God is mighty, but does not despise men; He is mighty, and firm in His purpose. (Job 9:4; 12:13; 36:5)

He does not keep the wicked alive but gives the afflicted their rights. He does not take His eyes off the righteous; He enthrones them with kings and exalts them forever. But if men are bound in chains, held fast by cords of affliction, He tells them what they have done — that they have sinned arrogantly. He makes them listen to correction and commands them to repent of their evil. If they obey and serve Him, they will spend the rest of their days in prosperity and their years in contentment. But if they do not listen, they will perish by the sword and die without knowledge. "The godless in heart harbor resentment; even when He fetters them, they do not cry for help. They die in their youth, among male prostitutes of the shrines. But those who suffer He delivers in their suffering; He speaks to them in their affliction. (Job 36:6-15)

Lift your eyes and look to the heavens: Who created all these? He who brings out the starry host one by one, and calls them each by name. Because of His great power and mighty strength, not one of them is missing. Why do you say, O Jacob, and complain, O Israel, "My way is hidden from the Lord; my cause is disregarded by my God"? Do you not know? Have you not heard? The Lord is the everlasting God, the Creator of the ends of the earth. He will not grow tired or weary, and His understanding no one can fathom. (Isa. 40:26-28)

"Praise be to the name of God for ever and ever; wisdom and power are His. He changes times and seasons; He sets up kings and deposes them. He gives wisdom to the wise and knowledge to the discerning. He reveals deep and hidden things; He knows what lies in darkness, and light dwells with Him." (Dan. 2:20)

Therefore, you kings, be wise; be warned, you rulers of the earth. Serve the Lord with fear and rejoice with trembling. Kiss the Son, lest He be angry and you be destroyed in your way, for His wrath can flare up in a moment. Blessed are all who take refuge in Him. (Psa. 2:10-12)

"The fear of the LORD is the beginning of wisdom, and knowledge of the Holy One is understanding."…The fear of the LORD is the beginning of knowledge, but fools despise wisdom and discipline…The fear of the LORD teaches a man wisdom…"The fear of the LORD— that is wisdom, and to shun evil is understanding." (Prov. 9:10; 1:7; 15:33; Job 28:28)

Then I said: "O LORD, God of heaven, the great and awesome God, who keeps His covenant of love with those who love Him and obey His commands,…"Don't be afraid of them. Remember the LORD, who is great and awesome…" "Now therefore, O our God, the great, mighty and awesome God, who keeps His covenant of love…" (Neh. 1:5; 4:14; 9:32)

Do not be terrified by them, for the Lord your God, who is among you, is a great and awesome God. For the Lord your God is God of gods and LORD of lords, the great God, mighty and awesome, who shows no partiality and accepts no bribes. He defends the cause of the fatherless and the widow, and loves the alien, giving him food and clothing. (Deut. 7:21; 10:17,18)

The LORD reigns, let the nations tremble; He sits enthroned between the cherubim, let the earth shake. Great is the Lord in Zion; He is exalted over all the nations. Let them praise Your great and awesome name—He is holy. The King is mighty, He loves justice—You have established equity; in Jacob You have done what is just and right. Exalt the LORD our God and worship at His footstool; He is holy. (Psa. 99:1-5)

But the LORD is with me like a mighty warrior; so my persecutors will stumble and not prevail. They will fail and be thoroughly disgraced; their dishonor will never be forgotten. O LORD Almighty, You who examine the righteous and probe the heart and mind, let me see Your vengeance upon them, for to You I have committed my cause. Sing to the Lord! Give praise to the Lord! He rescues the life of the needy from the hands of the wicked. (Jer. 20:11-13)

By the word of the LORD were the heavens made, their starry host by the breath of His mouth…For He spoke, and it came to be; He commanded, and it stood firm…By faith we understand that the universe was formed at God's command, so that what is seen was not made out of what was visible…But they deliberately forget that long ago by God's word the heavens existed and the earth was formed out of water and by water. (Psa. 33:6,9; Heb. 11:3; 2 Peter 3:5)

Praise the LORD. Praise God in His sanctuary; praise Him in His mighty heavens. Praise Him for His acts of power; praise Him for His surpassing greatness. Praise Him with the sounding of the trumpet, praise Him with the harp and lyre, praise Him with tambourine and dancing, praise Him with the strings and flute, praise Him with the clash of cymbals, praise Him with resounding cymbals. Let everything that has breath praise the LORD. Praise the LORD. (Psa. 150:1-6)

"For My thoughts are not your thoughts, neither are your ways My ways," declares the Lord. "As the heavens are higher than the earth, so are My ways higher than your ways and My thoughts than your thoughts. As the rain and the snow come down from heaven, and do not return to it without watering the earth and making it bud and flourish, so that it yields seed for the sower and bread for the eater, so is My word that goes out from My mouth: It will not return to Me empty, but will accomplish what I desire and achieve the purpose for which I sent it. (Isa. 55:8-11)

"Behold, I will create new heavens and a new earth. The former things will not be remembered, nor will they come to mind. But be glad and rejoice forever in what I will create, for I will create Jerusalem to be a delight and its people a joy. I will rejoice over Jerusalem and take delight in My people; the sound of weeping and of crying will be heard in it no more...They will not toil in vain or bear children doomed to misfortune; for they will be a people blessed by the Lord, they and their descendants with them. Before they call I will answer; while they are still speaking I will hear. The wolf and the lamb will feed together, and the lion will eat straw like the ox, but dust will be the serpent's food. They will neither harm nor destroy on all My holy mountain," says the Lord. (Isa. 65:17-19,23-25)

I will praise You, O LORD, among the nations; I will sing of You among the peoples. For great is Your love, higher than the heavens; Your faithfulness reaches to the skies. Be exalted, O God, above the heavens, and let Your glory be over all the earth. (Psa. 108:3-5)

The LORD is good to all; He has compassion on all He has made. All You have made will praise You, O LORD; Your saints will extol You. They will tell of the glory of Your kingdom and speak of Your might, so that all men may know of Your mighty acts and the glorious splendor of Your kingdom. Your kingdom is an everlasting kingdom, and Your dominion endures through all generations. The LORD is faithful to all His promises and loving toward all He has made. The LORD upholds all those who fall and lifts up all who are bowed down. The eyes of all look to You, and You give them their food at the proper time. (Psa. 145:9-15)

"Yet He has not left Himself without testimony: He has shown kindness by giving you rain from heaven and crops in their seasons; He provides you with plenty of food and fills your hearts with joy." (Acts 14:17)

"Far be it from You to do such a thing—to kill the righteous with the wicked, treating the righteous and the wicked alike. Far be it from You! Will not the Judge of all the earth do right?"…But it is God who judges: He brings one down, He exalts another. In the hand of the LORD is a cup full of foaming wine mixed with spices; He pours it out, and all the wicked of the earth drink it down to its very dregs…Rise up, O God, judge the earth, for all the nations are Your inheritance. (Gen. 18:25; Psa. 75:7-8; 82:8)

Then Peter said, "Ananias, how is it that Satan has so filled your heart that you have lied to the Holy Spirit and have kept for yourself some of the money you received for the land? Didn't it belong to you before it was sold? And after it was sold, wasn't the money at your disposal? What made you think of doing such a thing? You have not lied to men but to God." When Ananias heard this, he fell down and died. And great fear seized all who heard what had happened. (Acts 5:3-5)

On the appointed day Herod, wearing his royal robes, sat on his throne and delivered a public address to the people. They shouted, "This is the voice of a god, not of a man." Immediately, because Herod did not give praise to God, an angel of the Lord struck him down, and he was eaten by worms and died. (Acts 12:21-23)

But Elymas the sorcerer (for that is what his name means) opposed them and tried to turn the proconsul from the faith. Then Saul, who was also called Paul, filled with the Holy Spirit, looked straight at Elymas and said, "You are a child of the devil and an enemy of everything that is right! You are full of all kinds of deceit and trickery. Will you never stop perverting the right ways of the Lord? Now the hand of the LORD is against you. You are going to be blind, and for a time you will be unable to see the light of the sun." Immediately mist and darkness came over him, and he groped about, seeking someone to lead him by the hand. When the proconsul saw what had happened, he believed, for he was amazed at the teaching about the Lord. (Acts 13:8-12)

For anyone who eats and drinks without recognizing the body of the LORD eats and drinks judgment on himself. That is why many among you are weak and sick, and a number of you have fallen asleep. But if we judged ourselves, we would not come under judgment. When we are judged by the LORD, we are being disciplined so that we will not be condemned with the world. (1 Cor. 11:29-32)

Moreover, the Father judges no one, but has entrusted all judgment to the Son…"In my vision at night I looked, and there before me was one like a son of man, coming with the clouds of heaven. He approached the Ancient of Days and was led into His presence. He was given authority, glory and sovereign power; all peoples, nations and men of every language worshiped Him. His dominion is an everlasting dominion that will not pass away, and His kingdom is one that will never be destroyed." (John 5:22; Dan. 7:13-14)

"For He has set a day when He will judge the world with justice by the man He has appointed. He has given proof of this to all men by raising Him from the dead." (Acts 17:31)

"I do not rebuke you for your sacrifices or your burnt offerings, which are ever before me. I have no need of a bull from your stall or of goats from your pens, for every animal of the forest is mine, and the cattle on a thousand hills. I know every bird in the mountains, and the creatures of the field are mine. If I were hungry I would not tell you, for the world is mine, and all that is in it. Do I eat the flesh of bulls or drink the blood of goats? Sacrifice thank offerings to God, fulfill your vows to the Most High, and call upon Me in the day of trouble; I will deliver you, and you will honor Me." (Psa. 50:8-15)

Give thanks to the LORD, for He is good; His love endures forever. Let the redeemed of the Lord say this—those He redeemed from the hand of the foe…He delivered them from their distress. He led them by a straight way to a city where they could settle. Let them give thanks to the LORD for His unfailing love and His wonderful deeds for men, for He satisfies the thirsty and fills the hungry with good things. Some sat in darkness and the deepest gloom, prisoners suffering in iron chains, for they had rebelled against the words of God and despised the counsel of the Most High. So He subjected them to bitter labor; they stumbled, and there was no one to help. Then they cried to the Lord in their trouble, and He saved them from their distress. He brought them out of darkness and the deepest gloom and broke away their chains. (Psa. 107:1-2,6-14)

Shout with joy to God, all the earth! Sing the glory of His name; make His praise glorious! Say to God, "How awesome are Your deeds! So great is Your power that Your enemies cringe before You. All the earth bows down to You; they sing praise to You, they sing praise to Your name." *Selah* Come and see what God has done, how awesome His works in man's behalf! He turned the sea into dry land, they passed through the waters on foot — come, let us rejoice in Him. He rules forever by His power, His eyes watch the nations — let not the rebellious rise up against Him. *Selah* Praise our God, O peoples, let the sound of His praise be heard; He has preserved our lives and kept our feet from slipping. (Psa. 66:1-9)

You are resplendent with light, more majestic than mountains rich with game. Valiant men lie plundered, they sleep their last sleep; not one of the warriors can lift his hands. At Your rebuke, O God of Jacob, both horse and chariot lie still. You alone are to be feared. Who can stand before You when You are angry? From heaven You pronounced judgment, and the land feared and was quiet — when You, O God, rose up to judge, to save all the afflicted of the land. *Selah* Surely Your wrath against men brings You praise, and the survivors of Your wrath are restrained. (Psa. 76:4-10)

For to us a child is born, to us a son is given, and the government will be on His shoulders. And He will be called Wonderful Counselor, Mighty God, Everlasting Father, Prince of Peace. Of the increase of His government and peace there will be no end. He will reign on David's throne and over His kingdom, establishing and upholding it with justice and righteousness from that time on and forever. The zeal of the LORD Almighty will accomplish this. (Isa. 9:6-7)

"Holy, holy, holy is the LORD God almighty, who was, and is, and is to come." (Rev. 4:8)

✍

Please choose other Bible passages that reveal God's attributes to praise Him with in prayer. All of Scripture is inspired by God and reveals how great, loving, kind, just, holy, almighty, all present and all knowing He is, so do not stop with just the verses from these pages, but make the whole Bible the food of your praises. *He alone is worthy!*

An Overview of Verses That Reveal Our New Identity and Inheritance in Christ

Dear heavenly Father, we praise You for:

1. Shining Your light in our hearts to give us the knowledge of Christ. (2 Cor. 4:6)

2. Making us light in the LORD. (Eph. 5:8)

3. Rescuing us from darkness and bringing us into the kingdom of the Son. (Col. 1:13)

4. Giving Your one and only Son because You loved the world. (John 3:16)

5. Revealing a new righteousness that is by faith in Jesus Christ to all who believe. (Rom. 3:21,22)

6. Justifying the wicked who by faith trust in You. (Rom. 4:5)

7. Counting us righteous who believe in Christ's death and resurrection. (Rom. 4:18-25)

8. Giving us peace through the LORD Jesus Christ. (Rom. 5:1; John 14:27)

9. Pouring Your love into our hearts by the Holy Spirit, whom You gave us. (Rom. 5:5)

10. Giving Your Son to die for us while we were ungodly sinners. (Rom. 5:6-8)

11. Saving us from Your wrath through Him. (Rom. 5:9)

12. Bringing us near to You through the blood of Christ. (Eph. 2:13)

13. Reconciling us to Yourself through the LORD Jesus. (Rom. 5:11)

14. Giving us grace and righteousness to reign in life through one man, Your Son. (Rom. 5:17)

15. Burying us with Christ in death so that we too may live a new life. (Rom. 6:4)

16. Crucifying our old self with Christ to free us from the body of sin, in order that we may live with Him. (Rom. 6:5-8)

17. Making us alive to Yourself by Your mercy and grace. (Eph. 2:4,5)

18. Revealing this glorious mystery: Christ is in us, the hope of glory. (Col. 1:27)

19. Putting us in Christ and Him in us, just as He is in You. (John 14:20)

20. Making us new creations in Him. (2 Cor. 5:17)

21. Putting us under grace, not law, so that sin will not be our master. (Rom. 6:14)

22. Releasing us from the law so that we serve in the Spirit. (Rom. 7:4-6)

23. Rescuing us from the body of death through Jesus Christ, our LORD. (Rom. 7:24,25)

24. Giving us the Spirit, who enables us to meet the requirements of the law. (Rom. 8:4)

25. Setting us free in the Spirit, the purpose for which Christ came. (2 Cor. 3:17; Gal. 5:1)

26. Promising to give life to our mortal bodies through the Spirit when You raise us up with Christ. (Rom. 8:11; 2 Cor. 4:14)

27. Resurrecting us from the dead at the sound of the trumpet, when we will receive our new bodies. (1 Cor. 15:51,52)

28. Giving us victory over death through our Lord Jesus Christ. (1 Cor. 15:56,57)

29. Promising us a building, an eternal house in heaven, guaranteed by the Spirit. (2 Cor. 5:1,5)

30. Giving us the Spirit to intercede for us in accordance with Your will. (Rom. 8:26-27)

31. Working all things for our good because we love You and are called by Your purpose. (Rom. 8:28)

32. Predestining, calling, justifying, and glorifying us. (Rom. 8:29,30)

33. Being for us! Sparing not Your Son, who ever lives at Your side to intercede for us. (Rom. 8:31-34)

34. Making us stand firm in Christ through the anointing, deposit, and seal of the Spirit, who guarantees what is to come. (2 Cor. 1:21,22)

35. Making us strong to the end so that we will be blameless on the day of the Lord. (1 Cor. 1:8,9)

36. Creating us in Christ for good works which You prepared in advance. (Eph. 2:10)

37. Making us more than conquerors through Christ who loves us. (Rom. 8:37)

38. Always leading us in triumph in Christ and spreading His fragrance everywhere. (2 Cor. 2:14)

39. Allowing nothing to separate us from Your love—not death, or life, or angels or demons, or the present, or the future, or any powers, or height, or depth, or anything else in creation. (Rom. 8:38,39)

40. Giving us the right to be born of You when we believed in Christ and received Him. (John 1:12,13)

41. Including us in Christ when we believed, and marking us with a seal, the Holy Spirit, who guarantees our inheritance as Your possessions. (Eph. 1:13,14)

42. Giving us the Spirit of sonship, who testifies that we are Your children. (Rom. 8:15,16; Gal. 3:26; 4:6)

43. Lavishing Your love on us by calling us Your children and promising that when we see Him, we will be like Him. (1 John 3:1,2)

44. Making us not only Your children, but heirs of Yours and co-heirs with Christ. (Rom. 8:17)

45. Setting us free from slavery and making us sons with an inheritance. (Gal. 4:7)

46. Making us branches in the Vine, who is Christ. (John 15:5)

47. Giving us whatever we wish when we remain in Him and His words remain in us; making us fruitful. (John 15:5-7)

48. Making us friends of Your Son and enabling us to know everything He learned from You. (John 15:15)

49. Choosing us and appointing us to bear fruit that will last—then giving us whatever we ask in Christ's name. (John 15:16)

50. Setting us free from sin and making us slaves to righteousness. (Rom. 6:18)

51. Making us Your slaves so that we may reap holiness and eternal life. (Rom. 6:22)

52. Making Christ sin for us so that in Him we might become the righteousness of God. (2 Cor. 5:21)

53. Blessing us in heavenly realms with every spiritual blessing in Christ. (Eph. 1:3)

54. Raising us up with Christ and seating us in heaven. (Eph. 2:6,7)

55. Enabling us to die so that we might have a new life, hidden with Christ in You. (Col. 3:3)

56. Making us Your sons through our faith in Christ and clothing us with Him. (Gal. 3:26,27)

57. Baptizing us by one Spirit into one body. (1 Cor. 12:13)

58. Making us fellow citizens with Israel, members of one body, household, and dwelling, and sharers with them in the promise of Christ. (Eph. 2:19,22; 3:6)

59. Gifting us with different gifts and services by the Spirit and the Lord for the common good. (1 Cor. 12:4-7)

60. Making us members of Christ and temples of the Holy Spirit. (1 Cor. 3:16,17; 6:15,19)

61. Putting us in Christ, who is our wisdom, our righteousness, holiness, and redemption. (1 Cor. 1:30)

62. Giving us understanding of everything You have given us through the gift of the Spirit. (1 Cor. 2:12)

63. Giving us the mind of Christ. (1 Cor. 2:16)

64. Anointing us with the Holy Spirit, who teaches us all things. (1 John 2:20,27)

65. Choosing us before the creation of the world to be holy and blameless in Your sight. (Eph. 1:4, 11,12; John 15:19; 2 Th. 2:13)

66. Redeeming us from the curse of the law in order that we might receive the full rights of sons. (Gal. 3:13; 4:4,5)

67. Bringing us into the kingdom of the Son whom You love, in whom we have redemption. (Col. 1:14)

68. Redeeming us from an empty way of life with the precious blood of Christ, a Lamb without blemish or defect. (1 Peter 1:18)

69. Giving us the Counselor, the Spirit of truth, to be with us forever; He will be in us and with us, and through Him the Lord is with us too. (John 14:16-18)

70. Making us Your glorious inheritance. (Eph. 1:18)

71. Making us a chosen people, a royal priesthood, a holy people, and a kingdom to declare Your praises for taking us out of darkness, into Your wonderful light. (1 Peter 2:5,9)

72. Promising us that we will be priests of God and of Christ and will reign with Him for a thousand years. (Rev. 5:10; 20:6)

73. Keeping us from sin by our new birth and by the protection of Christ, so that the evil one cannot harm us. (1 John 5:18)

74. Giving us a spirit not of timidity, but of power, love and self-discipline. (2 Tim. 1:7)

75. Giving us Your Son as our intercessor so that we may approach Your throne with confidence to find grace and mercy. (Heb. 4:14-16)

76. Making us perfect forever through the sacrifice of the body of Jesus Christ, even as we are being made holy. (Heb. 10:14)

77. Enabling us to draw near to You by the blood and body of Jesus and through His priesthood. (Heb. 10:19-22)

78. Crushing Satan under our feet—soon; strengthening and protecting us from him. (Rom. 16:20; 2 Th. 3:3)

79. Inspiring the Scriptures and not letting them pass away. (2 Tim. 3:16-17; Matt. 24:35)

80. Being able to do more than all we can ask or even imagine. (Eph. 3:20-21)

81. Keeping us from falling and presenting us before Your presence without fault and with great joy. (Jude 24-25)

82. Giving us the new covenant. (Heb. 8:10-12)

83. Giving us a new birth into a living hope through Christ's resurrection, into an inheritance kept in heaven for us who are shielded by Your power. (1 Peter 1:3-5)

84. Making us alive when we were dead in sin; canceling the written code; disarming the rulers and authorities and triumphing over them by the cross. (Col. 2:13-15)

85. Giving us fullness in Christ. (Col. 2:9,10)

86. Promising us that the gates of hell will not prevail against the church. (Matt. 16:18)

87. Forgiving our sins when we confess them, and purifying us from all unrighteousness. (1 John 1:9)

88. Meeting all our needs through Your riches in glory in Christ Jesus. (Phil. 4:19)

PRAISING GOD FOR OUR NEW IDENTITY AND INHERITANCE IN CHRIST

For God, who said, "Let light shine out of darkness," made His light shine in our hearts to give us the light of the knowledge of the glory of God in the face of Christ...For you were once darkness, but now you are light in the Lord. (2 Cor. 4:6; Eph. 5:8)

> Dearest heavenly Father,
> Thank You for making Your light shine in our hearts to give us the knowledge of Christ, who is the glory of God! And thank You for making us light in Him!
> In the Light of the World, Jesus Christ, Amen

Giving thanks to the Father, who has qualified you to share in the inheritance of the saints in the kingdom of light. For He has rescued us from the dominion of darkness and brought us into the kingdom of the Son He loves. (Col. 1:12,13)

> Dear heavenly Father,
> How we thank You for rescuing us from the dominion of darkness and bringing us into the kingdom of Your dear Son, the kingdom of light! Thank You that He is the inheritance of all the saints, of everyone who believes.
> In the Son, Amen

"For God so loved the world that He gave His one and only Son, that whoever believes in Him shall not perish but have eternal life." (John 3:16)

> Dear heavenly Father,
> Thank You for giving Your Son and for enabling us to believe in Him and have eternal life. How can we ever thank You enough for the gift of Your Son and for the faith to receive Him? May our lives reflect our adoration and praise for Your wonderful grace.
> For the Savior's sake, Amen

But now a righteousness from God, apart from law, has been made known, to which the Law and the Prophets testify. This righteousness from God comes through faith in Jesus Christ to all who believe. There is no difference, for all have sinned and fall short of the glory of God, and are justified freely by His grace through the redemption that came by Christ Jesus. (Rom. 3:21-24)

> Dear heavenly Father,
> Thank You for giving us a new righteousness through our faith in Jesus Christ. Enable all who believe in Him to experience that they are right with You. Your grace through Christ has done it all!
>
> Because of Your Son, Amen

However, to the man who does not work but trusts God who justifies the wicked, his faith is credited as righteousness. (Rom. 4:5)

> Dear heavenly Father,
> Thank You for justifying us, the wicked, by enabling us to trust in You. Show us all, who call ourselves believers, that You justified us when we were wicked—even before we had done wicked things! We were wicked because we were born of Adam and participated in his sin and in his nature to sin. Remind us, too, that we were not saved by our works.
>
> In Christ, Amen

Against all hope, Abraham in hope believed and so became the father of many nations, just as it had been said to him, "So shall your offspring be." Without weakening in his faith, he faced the fact that his body was as good as dead — since he was about a hundred years old — and that Sarah's womb was also dead. Yet he did not waver through unbelief regarding the promise of God, but was strengthened in his faith and gave glory to God, being fully persuaded that God had power to do what He had promised. This is why "it was credited to him as righteousness." The words "it was credited to him" were written not for him alone, but also for us, to whom God will credit righteousness — for us who believe in Him who raised Jesus our LORD from the dead. He was delivered over to death for our sins and was raised to life for our justification. (Rom. 4:18-25)

Dear heavenly Father,

Thank You for our father, Abraham, who did not waver in unbelief but trusted You to do what You had promised. Thank You for putting to our credit the same righteousness of faith—that we believe that Christ died for our sins and was raised from the dead to make us right before You; He is our justification.

In Christ, our justifier, Amen

Therefore, since we have been justified through faith, we have peace with God through our LORD Jesus Christ…"Peace I leave with you; My peace I give you. I do not give to you as the world gives. Do not let your hearts be troubled and do not be afraid." (Rom. 5:1; John 14:27)

Dear heavenly Father,

Thank You for giving us peace through Christ. Enable us all to believe what You have done through Him and receive, by faith, the peace of God. He Himself is our peace—and He is in us!

In Christ, our peace, Amen

And hope does not disappoint us, because God has poured out His love into our hearts by the Holy Spirit, whom He has given us. (Rom. 5:5)

Dear heavenly Father,

Thank You for the love You have poured in our hearts that reassures us not only of right standing before You, but of depth of love. And thank You, too, for giving us the Holy Spirit, who is God in us, revealing this love to us!

In Christ, the love of God, Amen

You see, at just the right time, when we were still powerless, Christ died for the ungodly. Very rarely will anyone die for a righteous man, though for a good man someone might possibly dare to die. But God demonstrates His own love for us in this: while we were still sinners, Christ died for us. (Rom. 5:6-8)

Dear heavenly Father,

What would we have done, we who were powerless and ungodly, if

You had not given Your Son to die for us? What incredible love!
Open our eyes to understand Your grace, to marvel at Your love.

In Christ, Amen

Since we have now been justified by His blood, how much more shall we be saved from God's wrath through Him!...But now in Christ Jesus you who once were far away have been brought near through the blood of Christ. (Rom. 5:9; Eph. 2:13)

Dear heavenly Father,

We praise You that we have been saved from Your wrath because of His blood! Thank You for putting our sins on Your Son so that we would be saved from Your wrath! And thank You for bringing us near to You through His blood.

For the sake of Christ, who took Your wrath for us, Amen

Not only is this so, but we also rejoice in God through our Lord Jesus Christ, through whom we have now received reconciliation. (Rom. 5:11)

Dear heavenly Father,

We do rejoice because we are not only saved from wrath, but actually reconciled with You! Enable all believers to experience this reconciliation achieved by Christ.

For His sake, Amen

For if, by the trespass of the one man, death reigned through that one man, how much more will those who receive God's abundant provision of grace and of the gift of righteousness reign in life through the one man, Jesus Christ. (Rom. 5:17)

Dear heavenly Father,

Thank You for Your promise that we will reign in life through Christ Jesus! This does not depend on us, but upon Him! Thank You for Your abundant provision of grace!

In Christ, the man of grace, Amen

We were therefore buried with Him through baptism into death in order that, just as Christ was raised from the dead through the glory of the Father, we too may live a new life. (Rom. 6:4)

> Dear heavenly Father,
>
> This is a fact for which we give You praise: We were in Christ when He died and we, too, died. So that just as Christ was raised from the dead to glorify You, we too could glorify You by living a new life.
>
> For Your glory, Amen

If we have been united with Him like this in His death, we will certainly also be united with Him in His resurrection. For we know that our old self was crucified with Him so that the body of sin might be done away with, that we should no longer be slaves to sin—because anyone who has died has been freed from sin. Now if we died with Christ, we believe that we will also live with Him. (Rom. 6:5-8)

> Dear heavenly Father,
>
> When we died with Him, it was so the old "us" might be done away with so that we would no longer be compelled to sin, but rather to live a new life with Christ. How we praise You for delivering us from being enslaved to sin! How we thank You for the new life You have given us in Christ!
>
> In the name of our deliverer, Amen

In the same way, count yourselves dead to sin but alive to God in Christ Jesus...But because of His great love for us, God, who is rich in mercy, made us alive with Christ even when we were dead in transgressions—it is by grace you have been saved. (Rom. 6:11; Eph. 2:4,5)

> Dear heavenly Father,
>
> Thank You for making us alive to God by Your grace! Enable us to reckon ourselves (the old "us") dead to sin but alive to You in Christ. Thank You for this new life, which we have received because of Your great love for us.
>
> In Christ, Amen

To them God has chosen to make known among the Gentiles the glorious riches of this mystery, which is Christ in you, the hope of glory...On that day you will realize that I am in My Father, and you are in Me, and I am in you. (Col. 1:27; John 14:20)

> Dear heavenly Father,
>
> Enable us to comprehend that Christ is in us, and that You, too, are in us! God lives in us. How we praise You for living in our hearts!
>
> For Your glory, Amen

Therefore, if anyone is in Christ, he is a new creation; the old has gone, the new has come! (2 Cor. 5:17)

> Dear heavenly Father,
>
> Thank You for making me a new creation! Help me to accept this as a fact by faith, so that I will experience the truth of it in my daily life. Enable me to live as a new person. And may this glorious fact of newness of nature be revealed and appropriated by many in Your church.
>
> In Christ, Amen

For sin shall not be your master, because you are not under law, but under grace. (Rom. 6:14)

> Dear heavenly Father,
>
> Reveal to me this marvelous truth, that sin need never be my master because I am no longer under the letter of the law (the principle of law) but rather under grace! The new creation I have become through my death and resurrection with Christ loves to serve God! No longer, when I hear a command, is it my immediate desire to do the opposite, but rather, through the Spirit, it is my desire to obey it.
>
> Because of Your grace, Amen

So, my brothers, you also died to the law through the body of Christ, that you might belong to another, to Him who was raised from the dead, in order that we might bear fruit to God. For when we were controlled by the sinful nature, the sinful passions aroused by the law were at work in our bodies, so that we bore fruit for death. But now, by dying to what once bound us, we have been released from the law so that we serve in the new way of the Spirit, and not in the old way of the written code. (Rom. 7:4-6)

Dear heavenly Father,

How important it is to know and believe that we all died to the law so that we could belong to Christ! Direct our hearts and minds into an understanding of this truth. May we never relate to You under the letter of the law, but always by the Spirit, in Christ—so that we may bear fruit for You! This is what it means to "abide in Christ"!

Because of Your grace, Amen

...Who will rescue me from this body of death? Thanks be to God—through Jesus Christ our Lord!...(Rom. 7:24,25)

Dear heavenly Father,

Here again You show us the way of victory over sin—through the person who died for us and lives in us, Christ Jesus, the Lord! Only He can and will rescue us from the body of death we inhabit as long as we are on this earth. Whoever lives in Him will live victoriously; this is Your promise. Help us to believe it just as we believed Your promise about the gospel when we first came to Christ. Both are received by faith. Having begun by faith, enable us to go on to victory by faith.

In Christ, our victory, Amen

...in order that the righteous requirements of the law might be fully met in us, who do not live according to the sinful nature but according to the Spirit. (Rom. 8:4)

Dear heavenly Father,

Whoever lives by the Spirit naturally fulfills the requirements of the law! Enable us to believe this and to yield to His control. Thank You for Your gift of the Holy Spirit, who gives us the obedience of Christ within us!

In the One who is our obedience, Amen

Now the Lord is the Spirit, and where the Spirit of the LORD is, there is freedom...It is for freedom that Christ has set us free...(2 Cor. 3:17; Gal. 5:1)

> Dear heavenly Father,
>
> Thank You for the freedom that we have through the Spirit of Christ! Reveal to us this glorious freedom we have in Him and how fully You have provided for us.
>
> In the Spirit of the Lord, Amen

And if the Spirit of Him who raised Jesus from the dead is living in you, He who raised Christ from the dead will also give life to your mortal bodies through His Spirit, who lives in you...because we know that the one who raised the Lord Jesus from the dead will also raise us with Jesus and present us with you in His presence. (Rom. 8:11; 2 Cor. 4:14)

> Dear heavenly Father,
>
> And not only do we have Christ's life in us now, we also look forward to our resurrection bodies, when Your Spirit raises us from the dead even as He raised Christ from the dead! How we praise You for the certainty of our resurrection from the dead!
>
> In the One who is the Resurrection and the Life, Amen

Listen, I tell you a mystery: We will not all sleep, but we will all be changed—in a flash, in the twinkling of an eye, at the last trumpet. For the trumpet will sound, the dead will be raised imperishable, and we will be changed...The sting of death is sin, and the power of sin is the law. But thanks be to God! He gives us the victory through our LORD Jesus Christ. (1 Cor. 15:51,52,56,57)

> Dear heavenly Father,
>
> We will be changed into our new bodies, and the power of death will no longer hold us! We will have the victory of an imperishable, everlasting body through Jesus Christ the Lord! Praise God!
>
> In Christ, the Lord, Amen

Now we know that if the earthly tent we live in is destroyed, we have a building from God, an eternal house in heaven, not built by human hands...Now it is God who has made us for this very purpose and has given us the Spirit as a deposit, guaranteeing what is to come. (2 Cor. 5:1,5)

> Dear heavenly Father,
>
> You guarantee, by the Spirit You have given us, that You have waiting for us resurrection bodies, built by Your hands in heaven! How we look forward to that day when we shall finally be free of these bodies of sin, these tents of flesh we live in now!
>
> With eternal hope, Amen

In the same way, the Spirit helps us in our weakness. We do not know what we ought to pray for, but the Spirit Himself intercedes for us with groans that words cannot express. And He who searches our hearts knows the mind of the Spirit, because the Spirit intercedes for the saints in accordance with God's will. (Rom. 8:26,27)

> Dear heavenly Father,
>
> Thank You that the Holy Spirit enables us to pray when we do not know what to say. And He, being God, knows Your will and intercedes according to Your good pleasure. Thank You, Father, for giving us the blessed Holy Spirit to be in us.
>
> In the Spirit, who is the Lord, Amen

And we know that in all things God works for the good of those who love Him, who have been called according to His purpose. (Rom. 8:28)

> Dear heavenly Father,
>
> Thank You that everything in our lives will be worked out for good according to Your purpose, because You called us by Your love. May we all trust Your love! You will never do anything in our lives except what glorifies You and is good—eternally good—for us.
>
> For the love of God, Amen

For those God foreknew He also predestined to be conformed to the likeness of His Son, that He might be the firstborn among many brothers. And those He predestined, He also called; those He called, He also justified; those He justified, He also glorified. (Rom. 8:29,30)

> Dear heavenly Father,
>
> You predestined us to be like Your Son, so that He would have many brothers and sisters. Not only did You predestine us, You also called us to receive the gift of eternal life in Christ; then You justified us in Him—and the future is so certain: You promise us that we are already glorified! Open the eyes of our understanding, that we may comprehend how completely You have taken care of us—and will continue to take care of us! All this is not from us, but only from You.
>
> In the Son, who cannot fail, Amen

If God is for us, who can be against us? He who did not spare His own Son, but gave Him up for us all – how will He not also, along with Him, graciously give us all things? Who will bring any charge against those whom God has chosen? It is God who justifies. Who is He that condemns? Christ Jesus, who died – more than that, who was raised to life – is at the right hand of God and is also interceding for us. (Rom. 8:31-34)

> Dear heavenly Father,
>
> Enable us to believe this promise: Since You chose and justified us, and since Christ ever lives beside You to intercede for us by His blood, who can condemn us? We praise You, Father, that we are completely acceptable before You through Jesus Christ, the LORD. We praise You that You are "for" us and will give us all things along with Him.
>
> In Christ, who took our condemnation, Amen

Now it is God who makes both us and you stand firm in Christ. He anointed us, set His seal of ownership on us, and put His Spirit in our hearts as a deposit, guaranteeing what is to come. (2 Cor. 1:21,22)

Dear heavenly Father,

You make us stand firm! We count on You to do it. You have anointed us and sealed us, You own us, You have given us Your Spirit as a deposit, and You guarantee what is to come! We cannot fail!

Because of Your work in us, Amen

He will keep you strong to the end, so that you will be blameless on the day of our Lord Jesus Christ. God, who has called you into fellowship with His Son Jesus Christ our LORD, is faithful....For we are God's workmanship, created in Christ Jesus to do good works, which God prepared in advance for us to do. (1 Cor. 1:8,9; Eph. 2:10)

Dear heavenly Father,

Thank You for promising to keep us strong to the end—to make us blameless on the day of the Lord. Thank You that You created us in Christ to do good works, even preparing them in advance! We cannot fail because You won't let us.

Because of Your faithfulness, Amen

No, in all these things we are more than conquerors through Him who loved us. (Rom. 8:37)

Dear heavenly Father,

Thank You for making us more than conquerors through Christ, who loves us. Remind us to look to what is true—Your promises—and not to circumstances. Only Your Word gives us the grid of truth by which to make a correct assessment as to whether something is good or bad. By faith, we believe You and praise You for making us "more than conquerors"!

In the name of the Victor, Amen

But thanks be to God, who always leads us in triumphal procession in Christ and through us spreads everywhere the fragrance of the knowledge of Him. (2 Cor. 2:14)

Dearest Father,

Thank You for always making us triumphant in Christ and through us spreading everywhere the fragrance of the knowledge of Him! Praise You for enabling us to be that fragrance of Him.

In the fragrance of God, Christ Jesus, Amen

For I am convinced that neither death nor life, neither angels nor demons, neither the present nor the future, nor any powers, neither height nor depth, nor anything else in all creation, will be able to separate us from the love of God that is in Christ Jesus our LORD. (Rom. 8:38,39)

Dearest heavenly Father,

Is this not the essence of Your glorious gospel? Nothing can ever separate us from Your love to us in Christ Jesus, the Lord! We rejoice in Your love. We praise You for Your love—we thank You that no one and nothing can ever take it away from us!

In Christ, who has secured the Father's love, Amen

Yet to all who received Him, to those who believed in His name, He gave the right to become children of God—children born not of natural descent, nor of human decision or a husband's will, but born of God. (John 1:12,13)

Dear heavenly Father,

How we thank You that we are Your children—by Your will, not of human decision, but born of God! Reveal Yourself to us as our dearest Father, and enable us to please You because we are like You. May we grow up in faith and obedience like our brother Jesus! May it be said of us, "Like father, like son (or daughter)." And may this family resemblance be seen in as many children as possible in Your family.

For Christ's sake, Amen

And you also were included in Christ when you heard the word of truth, the gospel of your salvation. Having believed, you were marked in Him with a seal, the promised Holy Spirit, who is a deposit guaranteeing our inheritance until the redemption of those who are God's possession—to the praise of His glory. (Eph. 1:13,14)

Dear heavenly Father,

Thank You for marking us with a seal, the Holy Spirit, who guarantees our inheritance because we are God's possession. And no one can break that seal! We are Yours forever! We praise and thank You for Your wonderful gift.

Amen

For you did not receive a spirit that makes you a slave again to fear, but you received the Spirit of sonship. And by Him we cry, "*Abba*, Father." The Spirit Himself testifies with our spirit that we are God's children…You are all sons of God through faith in Christ Jesus…Because you are sons, God sent the Spirit of His Son into our hearts, the Spirit who calls out, "*Abba*, Father." (Rom. 8:15,16; Gal. 3:26; 4:6)

Dear Abba,

We are Your children! The Spirit You gave us the moment we believed in Christ bears witness with our spirits that we are Your children. We praise You! May You, blessed Holy Spirit, direct the hearts of all God's born-again children to rejoice over this blessed relationship with their Father in heaven, our Abba.

In Your Son, Amen

How great is the love the Father has lavished on us, that we should be called children of God! And that is what we are!…Dear friends, now we are children of God, and what we will be has not yet been made known. But we know that when He appears, we shall be like Him, for we shall see Him as He is. (1 John 3:1,2)

Dearest Father,

How much love You lavished on us when You made us Your children! How wonderful that we will see Jesus as He is—and be like Him! May this hope that is certain encourage our hearts.

For our brother Jesus' sake, Amen

Now if we are children, then we are heirs—heirs of God and co-heirs with Christ…So you are no longer a slave, but a son; and since you are a son, God has made you also an heir. (Rom. 8:17; Gal. 4:7)

Dear heavenly Father,

Show us what it means to be an heir with Christ! Does it not mean that You have given to us everything He has and is? That all Your riches in Him are now ours? Yes! And may we live as the spiritual millionaires You have made us to be. If we inherited a million dollars, wouldn't we be foolish if we lived as paupers? How much greater the wealth in Christ! Reveal to us how easily You can supply all our needs according to Your riches in glory in Christ Jesus! Amen

"I am the vine; you are the branches. If a man remains in Me and I in him, he will bear much fruit; apart from Me you can do nothing…If you remain in Me and My words remain in you, ask whatever you wish, and it will be given you. This is to My Father's glory, that you bear much fruit, showing yourselves to be My disciples." (John 15:5,7,8)

Dear heavenly Father,

Thank You for placing us in the Vine, who is Your Son. Enable us to remain in Him so that we bear much fruit. Show us the connection between Your Word in us and answered prayer; surely we must become people who have the Lord's heart, mind, and purposes for such a broad scope of "asking" and "answering" to be promised! Make us like Him by renewing our minds through the Word. We claim, too, that these promises are for all who are Your children. Reveal these truths to the whole body of Christ. Enable us all to bear fruit for Your glory.

In the Vine, Amen

I no longer call you servants, because a servant does not know his master's business. Instead, I have called you friends, for everything that I learned from My Father I have made known to you. (John 15:15)

Dear Lord Jesus,

We are now Your friends! Show us everything through the Bible and by Your Spirit of what You learned from Your Father. Make known to us our Father's business so that we, like You, will go about doing it.

For the Father's sake, Amen

You did not choose Me, but I chose you and appointed you to go and bear fruit—fruit that will last. Then the Father will give you whatever you ask in My name. (John 15:16)

> Dearest Lord Jesus,
>
> Thank You for choosing us and appointing us to bear fruit. You will not fail to make us fruitful, and the fruit will last. What a promise, too, that when we are fruitful, the Father will give us whatever we ask in Your name! Reveal these promises to the body of Christ worldwide for the Father's sake.
>
> In Your name, Amen

You have been set free from sin and have become slaves to righteousness. (Rom. 6:18)

> Dear heavenly Father,
>
> Oh, how we praise You that we are now, solely by Your grace and work, slaves of righteousness; this is true because we have a new nature like Yours and a new way of serving You—in the Spirit! Remind us of this truth so that by faith we will experience it. And reveal it to everyone who believes in Christ, for His sake.
>
> Because of the One who set us free, Amen

But now that you have been set free from sin and have become slaves to God, the benefit you reap leads to holiness, and the result is eternal life. (Rom. 6:22)

> Dearest Father,
>
> Does a slave have any choice in what he does? No. And may this be true of us and all believers. May we find ourselves enslaved to God, becoming holy and reaping eternal life.
>
> In Christ Jesus, Amen

God made Him who had no sin to be sin for us, so that in Him we might become the righteousness of God. (2 Cor. 5:21)

Dear heavenly Father,

What grace! You made Jesus become an object of our sin so that in Him we might become the very righteousness of God! And we had nothing to do with any of it! Enable us to believe what You have already done.

Because of Your Son, Amen

Praise be to the God and Father of our Lord Jesus Christ, who has blessed us in the heavenly realms with every spiritual blessing in Christ. (Eph. 1:3)

Dear heavenly Father,

Thank You for giving us every spiritual blessing in Christ! Enable us to believe that this is true and by faith release these blessings in our daily lives. Amen

And God raised us up with Christ and seated us with Him in the heavenly realms in Christ Jesus, in order that in the coming ages He might show the incomparable riches of His grace, expressed in His kindness to us in Christ Jesus…For you died, and your life is now hidden with Christ in God. (Eph. 2:6-7; Col. 3:3)

Dear heavenly Father,

Open our eyes to believe that we died and You raised us up in heaven, seated us with Christ, and have given us a new life, hidden with Him in You. How we praise You for Your incomparable grace to us in Him!

For Your glory, Amen

You are all sons of God through faith in Christ Jesus, for all of you who were baptized into Christ have clothed yourselves with Christ. There is neither Jew nor Greek, slave nor free, male nor female, for you are all one in Christ Jesus…For we were all baptized by one Spirit into one body— whether Jews or Greeks, slave or free—and we were all given the one Spirit to drink…Now you are the body of Christ, and each one of you is a part of it. (Gal. 3:26-28; 1 Cor. 12:13,27)

Dear heavenly Father,

Thank You for our oneness in Christ! All the divisions are gone. Through the Holy Spirit we are part of Christ and members of His body. Enable us to comprehend this unity, which is the same as Yours with the Son.

So that the world may believe in Christ, Amen

Therefore, remember that formerly you who are Gentiles by birth…were separate from Christ, excluded from citizenship in Israel and foreigners to the covenants of the promise,…But now in Christ Jesus you who once were far away have been brought near through the blood of Christ…Consequently, you are no longer foreigners and aliens, but fellow citizens with God's people and members of God's household,…And in Him you too are being built to become a dwelling in which God lives by His Spirit…through the gospel the Gentiles are heirs together with Israel, and members together of one body, and sharers together in the promise in Christ Jesus. (Eph. 2:11-13,19,22; 3:6)

Dear heavenly Father,

Thank You for including us Gentiles in Your household of faith! Thank You for bringing us near to the Jews through the blood of Christ! Thank You for making us, together with them, Your dwelling place and for making both of us joint-heirs in the promise of Christ.

In the Messiah, Amen

There are different kinds of gifts, but the same Spirit. There are different kinds of service, but the same Lord. There are different kinds of working, but the same God works all of them in all men. Now to each one the manifestation of the Spirit is given for the common good. (1 Cor. 12:4-7)

Dear heavenly Father,

Thank You for giving us gifts by the Spirit, to be used in different kinds of services to benefit the body of Christ, of which we are all a part. And thank You that You work them in all men! One God, one Lord, one Spirit, gifting all of us for the common good.

With thanksgiving, Amen

Do you not know that your bodies are members of Christ Himself?…Do you not know that your body is a temple of the Holy Spirit, who is in you, whom you have received from God?…Don't you know that you yourselves are God's temple and that God's Spirit lives in you? If anyone destroys God's temple, God will destroy him; for God's temple is sacred, and you are that temple. (1 Cor. 6:15,19; 3:16,17)

> Dearest Holy Father,
>
> We are members of Christ Himself, and our bodies are temples of the Holy Spirit, who is God. This is awesome and wonderful—that You have made Your habitation in us!
>
> For Your glory, Amen

It is because of Him that you are in Christ Jesus, who has become for us wisdom from God—that is, our righteousness, holiness and redemption. (1 Cor. 1:30)

> Dear heavenly Father,
>
> It is from You that we are "in" Christ; You placed us in Him. He is our wisdom, our righteousness, our holiness and redemption. Did we have anything to do with our union with Christ? No. Then, just as surely as it was by faith that we received Christ to begin with, surely it is by faith that we will grow! Enable us to trust that You will give us all we need from Him for our sanctification, righteousness and redemption. It is all from You, through Him.
>
> In Christ, our life, Amen

We have not received the spirit of the world but the Spirit who is from God, that we may understand what God has freely given us…"For who has known the mind of the Lord that he may instruct Him?" But we have the mind of Christ. (1 Cor. 2:12,16)

> Dear heavenly Father,
>
> We have the mind of our Lord! The Holy Spirit You have given us enables us to understand what You have freely given us. This is awesome and wonderful! Thank You for enabling us to know You.
>
> With praise, Amen

But you have an anointing from the Holy One...As for you, the anointing you received from Him remains in you, and you do not need anyone to teach you. But as His anointing teaches you about all things and as that anointing is real, not counterfeit—just as it has taught you, remain in Him. (1 John 2:20,27)

> Dear heavenly Father,
>
> Because of the blessed Holy Spirit, we are able to understand all things of Christ. Thank You that this anointing is real and not a counterfeit! Enable us to remain in Him because of it.
>
> For His sake, Amen

For He chose us in Him before the creation of the world to be holy and blameless in His sight...In Him we were also chosen, having been predestined according to the plan of Him who works out everything in conformity with the purpose of His will,...I have chosen you out of the world...from the beginning God chose you to be saved...(Eph. 1:4,11,12; John 15:19; 2 Th. 2:13)

> Dear heavenly Father,
>
> Thank You for choosing us to be saved out of the world and unto holiness. Make all of us who have been chosen grateful and thankful. And enable us to realize this was based on Your choice, not our worthiness! May we be humbled, not made proud, by such marvelous grace!
>
> For the sake of Christ Jesus, Amen

Christ redeemed us from the curse of the law by becoming a curse for us,...But when the time had fully come, God sent His Son, born of a woman, born under law, to redeem those under law, that we might receive the full rights of sons...[He] brought us into the kingdom of the Son He loves, in whom we have redemption, the forgiveness of sins...For you know that it was not with perishable things such as silver or gold that you were redeemed from the empty way of life handed down to you from your forefathers, but with the precious blood of Christ, a lamb without blemish or defect. (Gal. 3:13; 4:4-5; Col. 1:13,14; 1 Peter 1:18,19)

Dear heavenly Father,

We have been redeemed from the curse of the law by Your precious Son, the Lord, that we might be sons of Yours and live in Your kingdom. It was His precious blood that redeemed us from an empty way of life. May we never forget what it cost our beloved Savior to purchase us out from under the curse we deserved! We thank You and worship You for our redemption through His blood.

In our wonderful Lord, Amen

And I will ask the Father, and He will give you another Counselor to be with you forever—the Spirit of truth. The world cannot accept Him, because it neither sees Him nor knows Him. But you know Him, for He lives with you and will be in you. I will not leave you as orphans; I will come to you. (John 14:16-18)

Dear Father,

Thank You for the blessed Holy Spirit, who makes us one with Jesus! We are not alone. The Lord is in us and with us.

In Christ, Amen

I pray also that the eyes of your heart may be enlightened in order that you may know the hope to which He has called you, the riches of His glorious inheritance in the saints. (Eph. 1:18)

Dear heavenly Father,

Open our hearts to comprehend that You, also, have an inheritance in us—that we will bring You glory because we are saints of God! We praise You that we will, through Christ, offer You good works.

For Your sake, Amen

You also, like living stones, are being built into a spiritual house to be a holy priesthood, offering spiritual sacrifices acceptable to God through Jesus Christ…But you are a chosen people, a royal priesthood, a holy nation, a people belonging to God, that you may declare the praises of Him who called you out of darkness into His wonderful light…"You have made them to be a kingdom and priests to serve our God, and they will reign on the earth."…they will be priests of God and of Christ and will reign with

Him for a thousand years. (1 Peter 2:5,9; Rev. 5:10; 20:6)

> Dear heavenly Father,
> You have made us a holy and royal priesthood, offering spiritual sacrifices to God through Christ! We do praise Your name, Father, for taking us out of darkness and bringing us into Your wonderful light! And we look forward to reigning on earth as Your priests, to serve You and Christ for a thousand years!
>
> For the glory of God, Amen

We know that anyone born of God does not continue to sin; the one who was born of God keeps him safe, and the evil one cannot harm him. (1 John 5:18)

> Dear heavenly Father,
> Thank You that we will not continue to sin because we have been born of God, and thank You that Jesus will keep us safe from the Evil One. He cannot harm us! Amen

For God did not give us a spirit of timidity, but a spirit of power, of love and of self-discipline. (2 Tim. 1:7)

> Dear heavenly Father,
> Thank You for giving us the Holy Spirit—the Spirit who enables our spirits to be unafraid, powerful, loving and self-disciplined!
>
> In Christ, our life, Amen

Therefore, since we have a great high priest who has gone through the heavens, Jesus the Son of God, let us hold firmly to the faith we profess. For we do not have a high priest who is unable to sympathize with our weaknesses, but we have one who has been tempted in every way, just as we are—yet was without sin. Let us then approach the throne of grace with confidence, so that we may receive mercy and find grace to help us in our time of need. (Heb. 4:14-16)

> Dear heavenly Father,
> Thank You for our high priest, the Lord, who sympathizes with our weaknesses and gives us mercy and grace when we need it.
>
> Amen

…we have been made holy through the sacrifice of the body of Jesus Christ once for all…because by one sacrifice He has made perfect forever those who are being made holy. (Heb. 10:10,14)

> Dearest Lord Jesus,
>
> Thank You that by Your sacrifice You have made us perfect forever, even as we are being made holy. We have been justified and are being sanctified—all by Christ Jesus, our Lord.
>
> Because of Christ, Amen

Therefore, brothers, since we have confidence to enter the Most Holy Place by the blood of Jesus, by a new and living way opened for us through the curtain, that is, His body, and since we have a great priest over the house of God, let us draw near to God with a sincere heart in full assurance of faith, having our hearts sprinkled to cleanse us from a guilty conscience and having our bodies washed with pure water. (Heb. 10:19-22)

> Dear heavenly Father,
>
> Thank You for the blood of Your Son and for His great priesthood, which has opened up a new way into Your presence and enables us to draw near to You with confidence.
>
> In Christ, our high priest, Amen

The God of peace will soon crush Satan under your feet. The grace of our Lord Jesus be with you…But the Lord is faithful, and He will strengthen and protect you from the evil one. (Rom. 16:20; 2 Th. 3:3)

> Dearest heavenly Father,
>
> Thank You for these promises, that You will soon crush Satan under our feet and that You will strengthen and protect us from him.
>
> In Christ, the Victor, Amen

All Scripture is God-breathed and is useful for teaching, rebuking, correcting and training in righteousness, so that the man of God may be thoroughly equipped for every good work…Heaven and earth will pass away, but My words will never pass away. (2 Tim. 3:16,17; Matt. 24:35)

Dear heavenly Father,

How can we ever thank You enough for giving us Your very words! How we praise You and thank You for the Bible.

In Christ, our life, Amen

Now to Him who is able to do immeasurably more than all we ask or imagine, according to His power that is at work within us, to Him be the glory in the church and in Christ Jesus throughout all generations, for ever and ever! Amen (Eph. 3:20,21).

Dear heavenly Father,

Thank You for the power at work within us through which You are able to do more than we can even ask or imagine! Oh, may we dare to trust in You by asking You for things that seem beyond what You would do—for Your glory. Amen

To Him who is able to keep you from falling and to present you before His glorious presence without fault and with great joy—to the only God our Savior be glory, majesty, power and authority, through Jesus Christ our Lord, before all ages, now and forevermore! Amen (Jude 24,25)

Dearest Father,

Thank You that You are able to keep us from falling and to present us before You without fault and with great joy. And thank You that You will!

With thanksgiving, Amen

"This is the covenant I will make with the house of Israel after that time, declares the LORD. I will put My laws in their minds and write them on their hearts. I will be their God, and they will be My people. No longer will a man teach his neighbor, or a man his brother, saying, 'Know the LORD,' because they will all know Me, from the least of them to the greatest. For I will forgive their wickedness and will remember their sins no more." (Heb. 8:10-12)

Dear heavenly Father,

Thank You for the new covenant, in which You have done for us

what we could not do for ourselves; forgiven our sins and wickedness and enabled us not to continue sinning. May we live out the
new covenant by living by the Spirit, revealing the Son's life.

For His sake, Amen

Praise be to the God and Father of our LORD Jesus Christ! In His great
mercy He has given us new birth into a living hope through the resurrection of Jesus Christ from the dead, and into an inheritance that can never
perish, spoil or fade—kept in heaven for you, who through faith are shielded
by God's power until the coming of the salvation that is ready to be revealed in the last time. (1 Peter 1:3-5)

Dear Father in heaven,

Thank You for giving us birth into a living hope through Christ's
resurrection, into an inheritance in heaven that can't perish, spoil
or fade! And thank You for shielding us by Your power until the
coming day of salvation, which will be revealed in the last times.

With thanksgiving, Amen

When you were dead in your sins and in the uncircumcision of your sinful
nature, God made you alive with Christ. He forgave us all our sins, having
canceled the written code, with its regulations, that was against us and that
stood opposed to us; He took it away, nailing it to the cross. And having
disarmed the powers and authorities, He made a public spectacle of them,
triumphing over them by the cross. (Col. 2:13-15)

Dearest Father,

We praise You for making us alive with Your Son, forgiving our
sins, canceling the written code that was against us and nailing it
to the cross, and disarming the devil and his forces—triumphing
over them by the cross! What victory You have given us!

Because of the Victor, Christ Jesus, Amen

For in Christ all the fullness of the Deity lives in bodily form, and you have
been given fullness in Christ, who is the head over every power and authority. (Col. 2:9,10)

Dear heavenly Father,

You gave Jesus the victory over the devil and his forces because He is God in bodily form, who died for our sins and was raised for our life. In Him we have fullness! And in Him we are also over every power and authority!

> In the fullness of Christ, Amen

"And I tell you that you are Peter, and on this rock I will build My church, and the gates of Hades will not overcome it." (Matt. 16:18)

Dear mighty Father,

We praise You that You will build Your church, and the gates of hell will never overcome it! And we who believe and have received Your Son are the church. Protect us all.

> In the mighty One, Amen

If we confess our sins, He is faithful and just and will forgive us our sins and purify us from all unrighteousness. (1 John 1:9)

Dear Holy Father,

Thank You for being faithful to Your Son's blood and work at Calvary by forgiving and cleansing us from all unrighteousness when we agree with You that we have sinned. Thank You that He paid the penalty so that we do not have to pay it!

> For the Lord's sake, Amen

And my God will meet all your needs according to His glorious riches in Christ Jesus. (Phil. 4:19)

Dearest Father,

Thank You for meeting all our needs through Your riches in Christ Jesus. In Him we have been made rich in every way.

> In Christ, our inheritance, Amen

Praising God for Who I Am in Christ

I praise You, heavenly Father, that in Christ:

1. I am the object of Your love. (Rom. 5:6-8; John 3:16)

2. I am born again. (John 1:12,13)

3. I am Your child. (Rom. 8:15,16; Gal. 3:26; 4:6; 1 John 3:1,2)

4. I am an heir with Christ. (Rom. 8:17; Gal. 4:7)

5. I am chosen. (Eph. 1:4,11,12; John 15:19; 2 Th. 2:13)

6. I am forgiven. (Eph. 1:7)

7. I am justified. (Rom. 3:21-24; 4:5)

8. I am redeemed. (Col. 1:14; Gal. 3:13; 4:4,5; 1 Peter 1:18)

9. I am holy. (Heb. 10:10)

10. I am right with God. (Rom. 3:21-24; 4:18-25)

11. I am certain that God is for me. (Rom. 8:31,32)

12. I am near to God. (Eph. 2:13)

13. I am not alone. (John 14:16-18)

14. I am a friend of God. (John 15:15)

15. I am saved from wrath. (Rom. 5:9)

16. I am reconciled to God. (Rom. 5:11)

17. I am at peace with God. (Rom. 5:1; John 14:27)

18. I am a new creation. (2 Cor. 5:17)

19. I am not bound by sin. (Rom. 6:4-8)

20. I am not under the principle of law. (Rom. 6:14)

21. I am Christ's. (Rom. 7:4-6)

22. I am a Christian. (Col. 1:27; John 14:20)

23. I am in Christ. (John 14:20; Eph. 1:13; 1 Cor. 1:30; 1 John 5:20b)

24. I am free. (2 Cor. 3:17; Gal. 5:1)

25. I am free from this body of death. (Rom. 7:24,25)

26. I am no longer condemned. (Rom. 8:33,34)

27. I am alive. (Rom. 6:11; Eph. 2:4,5)

28. I am sealed by the Holy Spirit. (Eph. 1:13,14)

29. I am a saint. (Eph. 1:18)

30. I am a slave to God and to righteousness. (Rom. 6:18,22)

31. I am the very righteousness of God. (2 Cor. 5:21)

32. I am raised up in heaven. (Eph. 2:6-10; Col. 3:3)

33. I am a branch in the Vine, who is Christ. (John 15:5,7,8)

34. I am predestined, called, justified and glorified. (Rom. 8:30)

35. I am blessed with all spiritual blessings. (Eph. 1:3)

36. I am more than a conqueror. (Rom. 8:37)

37. I am always triumphant. (2 Cor. 2:14)

38. I am powerful. (2 Tim. 1:7)

39. I am strong. (1 Cor. 1:8,9)

40. I am chosen and appointed to bear fruit. (John 15:16)

41. I am able to stand firm. (2 Cor. 1:21,22)

42. I am a temple of God. (1 Cor. 3:16,17; 6:19)

43. I am a member of Christ, part of His body. (1 Cor. 6:15; 12:13)

44. I am one with the other members of His body. (1 Cor. 12:12,13,25,27)

45. I am gifted by God for the sake of the body. (1 Cor. 12:4-7)

46. I am a child of light. (Eph. 5:8)

47. I am in the kingdom of the Son. (Col. 1:12,13)

48. I am victorious over death. (1 Cor. 15:51,52,56,57)

49. I am God's inheritance. (Eph. 1:18)

50. I am God's workmanship. (Eph. 2:10)

51. I am a member of God's household with Israel. (Eph. 2:11-13,19)

52. I am a dwelling for God. (Eph. 2:22)

53. I am an heir with Israel in Christ. (Eph. 3:6)

54. I am a priest. (1 Peter 2:5,9; Rev. 5:10; 20:6)

55. I am able to understand what God has given me. (1 Cor. 2:12,16)

56. I am anointed by God with the Holy Spirit. (1 John 2:20,27)

57. I am victorious over the evil one. (1 John 5:18)

58. I am an ambassador of Christ. (2 Cor. 5:20)

59. I am God's possession. (Eph. 1:14)

60. I am full of God. (Col. 2:9)

61. I am Your beloved. (John 14:21)

62. I am being transformed into Christlikeness. (2 Cor. 3:18)

63. I am being renewed in knowledge in Your image. (Col. 3:10)

64. I am light. (Matt. 5:14)

65. I am salt. (Matt. 5:13)

66. I am an alien and a stranger in this world. (1 Peter 2:11)

67. I am an enemy of the devil. (1 Peter 5:8)

68. I am a brother of the Son. (Heb. 2:11)

69. I am shielded by God's power. (1 Peter 1:5)

70. I am able to participate in the divine nature through Your promises. (2 Peter 1:4)

71. I am competent as a minister of the new covenant. (2 Cor. 3:6)

72. I am like Him in this world. (1 John 4:17)

PERSONAL PRAISE AND THANKSGIVING

Journal or remember what God has done and is doing in your life, in your family, in your church, in the Body of Christ, in your community and in the world.

Personal Praise and Thanksgiving

PERSONAL PRAISE AND THANKSGIVING

PERSONAL PRAISE AND THANKSGIVING

PERSONAL PRAISE AND THANKSGIVING

PERSONAL PRAISE AND THANKSGIVING

CONFESSION
OF SIN

If we confess our sins, He is faithful and just and will forgive us
our sins and purify us from all unrighteousness.
1 John 1:9

Confession of Sin

There are six chapters on confessing sin and interceding on behalf of others who have sinned:

1. *Commandments of God That Convict Us of Sin* – verses that reveal God's standard and convict us of sin.
2. *Convict Me of My Sins* – Prayers that will help you recognize areas of sin in your life.
3. *My Personal Confession of Sin* – A place for confession of your personal sin.
4. *Interceding for the Sins of My Family* – Prayers on behalf of the sins of your loved ones.
5. *Interceding for the Sins of the Church at Large* – Intercessory prayer for all Christians around the world.
6. *Interceding for the Sins of My Local Church* – Confession for the sins of your local church, asking God to bring conviction, repentance and restoration.

How to Use This Section

Start by reading daily the first chapter, *Commandments of God That Convict Us of Sin*, which lays out God's standards for all of life and godliness. These commandments sum up what God requires of us, His people. Whenever we don't obey them, we have sinned.

Next, go to the *Convict Me of My Sins* chapter. This chapter seeks to bring conviction of sin through the application of God's commandments in the different areas of one's life.

Next, go to the chapter *My Personal Confession of Sin*, which is a place to confess your own sins to God.

Having been made right with God through your own confession of sin, turn to the *Interceding for the Sins of My Family* chapter to come before God to intercede for the sins of your loved ones.

This section concludes with two chapters: *Interceding for the Sins of the Church at Large* and *Interceding for the Sins of My Local Church*.

DEFINING THE CONCEPTS OF SIN, CONFESSION AND INTERCESSION

What Is Sin?

Sin is unbelief in and disobedience to the God of the Holy Scriptures. All sin springs from not acknowledging or honoring God. In Romans, God tells us through the apostle Paul:

> For since the creation of the world God's invisible qualities—His eternal power and divine nature—have been clearly seen, being understood from what has been made, so that men are without excuse. For although they knew God, they neither glorified Him as God nor gave thanks to Him, but their thinking became futile and their foolish hearts were darkened. (Rom. 1:20,21)

And in the book of Hebrews, God tells us how we must come to Him:

> And without faith it is impossible to please God, because anyone who comes to Him must believe that He exists and that He rewards those who earnestly seek Him. (Heb. 11:6)

The first of the Ten Commandments expresses this same truth: "You shall have no other gods before Me." (Ex. 20:3) The root of all sin, therefore, is unbelief:

> This righteousness from God comes through faith in Jesus Christ to all who believe. There is no difference, for all have sinned and fall short of the glory of God, and are justified freely by His grace through the redemption that came by Christ Jesus. (Rom. 3:22-24)

Not only is the way to God initially by faith in the Lord Jesus Christ; it is also the way we are to continue to come to Him: "The righteous will live by faith" (Rom. 1:17). All sin springs from an improper relationship with God. Jesus said, "'Love the Lord your God with all your heart and with all your soul and with all your mind.' This is the first and greatest commandment" (Matt. 22:37,38). In Revelation 2:4-5, God tells us through the apostle John, "Yet I hold this against you: You have forsaken your first love. Remember the height from which you have fallen!" (emphasis added). God, who is our creator and the creator of all things (Rev. 4:11), requires our love and devotion and has given His Son in order to bring us into a love relationship with Himself. It is through Christ—and only through Christ—that we are able to find and live in the love of God.

How does loving God express itself? Jesus said:

> "Whoever has My commands and obeys them, he is the one who loves Me. He who loves Me will be loved by My Father, and I too will love him and show myself to him…"If anyone loves Me, he will obey My teaching. My Father will love him, and we will come to him and make our home with him." (John 14:21,23)

Genuine faith in and love for Jesus Christ is expressed in obedience to God's commands.

> We know that we have come to know Him if we obey His commands. The man who says, "I know Him," but does not do what He commands is a liar, and the truth is not in him. But if anyone obeys His word, God's love is truly made complete in him. (1 John 2:3-5)

What Is Confession of Sin, and Why Does God Require It?

To confess sin means to agree with God that one has failed to love and obey Him by faith in Jesus Christ. Someone who confesses his sin is acknowledging his guilt (Lev. 5:5; Psa. 32:5). It is the specific ministry of the Holy Spirit to convict of sin through the Scriptures, because it is through the Scriptures that we become conscious of sin (John 16:8; 17:17; Rom. 3:20). God requires us to confess our sin—to agree with Him about it—in order to deliver us from it. He gave His Son to deliver us from bondage to sin, that we might be slaves of God:

> But now that you have been set free from sin and have become slaves to God, the benefit you reap leads to holiness, and the result is eternal life. (Rom. 6:22)

Therefore, while it is true that whoever has received salvation as a gift of grace from God by faith in Jesus Christ has been made forever perfect, it is also true that we are in the process of being made holy (Heb. 10:10,14). In Hebrews 10:14, God tells us, "…by one sacrifice [Christ] has made perfect forever those who are being made holy." This verse contrasts our position in Christ (our being made perfect forever through faith in Him) with our walk with Him over a lifetime (our being made holy through that same faith). 1 John 3:6 says, "No one who lives in Him keeps on sinning. No one who continues to sin has either seen Him or known Him." Yet listen to 1 John 1:8-10:

> If we claim to be without sin, we deceive ourselves and the truth is not in us. If we confess our sins, He is faithful and just and will forgive us our sins and purify us from all unrighteousness. If we claim we have not sinned, we make Him out to be a liar and his word has no place in our lives.

God is plainly telling us that while Christians should not continue in patterns of sin because they have been delivered from the power of sin and of law, they will still sin (Rom. 6:4-8,18,22; 7:4-6). When they do sin, they need to confess it in order to receive forgiveness and purification from God. Therefore, confession is essential to maintaining fellowship with God, not right standing before God.

In 1 John 1:9, God is called "faithful" and "just" to forgive us when we confess (that is, when we agree with Him that we have transgressed His commandments) because Jesus has already paid for that sin by His death on the cross. God is therefore faithful to the work of His Son. He does not punish us because Christ was already punished. But He does require confession so that we might once again enjoy fellowship with Him. God cannot fellowship with those who break His commandments (Isa. 59:2; John 14:21)! Personal confession, as commanded in 1 John 1:9, therefore includes the concept of repentance: a genuine sorrow to God for sinning and a genuine desire not to sin again (2 Cor. 7:9,10; Matt. 5:3,4).

Why Is Personal Confession of Sin So Important for Those Who Want Their Prayers Answered?

According to Scripture, God only hears the prayers of the righteous, and it is the prayers of the righteous person that God answers:

> But your iniquities have separated you from your God; your sins have hidden His face from you, so that He will not hear. (Isa. 59:2)

> The prayer of a righteous man is powerful and effective. (James 5:16b)

> "For the eyes of the Lord are on the righteous and His ears are attentive to their prayer, but the face of the Lord is against those who do evil." (1 Peter 3:12)

Moreover, the Lord's promises to believers about answered prayer are conditional upon their obeying His commands: "If you remain in Me and My words remain in you, ask whatever you wish, and it will be given you." (John 15:7). We will not remain in Him unless we obey His commands:

> "Whoever has My commands and obeys them, he is the one who loves Me. He who loves Me will be loved by My Father, and I too will love him and show myself to him…If anyone loves Me, he will obey My teaching. My Father will love him, and we will come to him and make our home with him." (John 14:21,23)

What Scriptural Support Is There for Interceding for the Sins of Other People?

While only Christ actually intercedes for the world (all of humanity) since He "made intercession for the transgressors." (Isa. 53:12), "…is the atoning sacrifice for our sins, and not only for ours but also for the sins of the whole world." (1 John 2:2), and "…gave Himself as a ransom for all men…" (1 Tim. 2:6) and especially for those who believe (John 17:9; 1 Tim. 4:10), the validity of human intercession for others through prayer is illustrated in both the Old and New Testaments.

When we intercede on behalf of the sins of others, we are not absolving anyone of guilt. God holds each person accountable for his own sin (Ezek. 18:4; Jer. 31:30). The only way one can be absolved of guilt for sin is through his own repentance. Therefore, when we intercede on behalf of the sins of others, we are asking God to enable them to come to their own repentance.

It is the thesis of this book that it is this role of the intercessor that has largely been lost or insufficiently appropriated by believers. God has made us to be a royal priesthood:

> But you are a chosen people, a royal priesthood, a holy nation, a people belonging to God, that you may declare

the praises of Him who called you out of darkness into His wonderful light. (1 Peter 2:9)

"You have made them to be a kingdom and priests to serve our God, and they will reign on the earth." (Rev. 5:10)

In 1 Peter 2:5, God tells us, "You also, like living stones, are being built into a spiritual house to be a holy priesthood, offering spiritual sacrifices acceptable to God through Jesus Christ." On what basis does this priesthood rest? It rests on the basis of our union with Christ, our High Priest: "On that day you will realize that I am in My Father, and you are in Me, and I am in you." (John 14:20). God the Father has placed us in Him (1 Cor. 1:30; 1 John 5:20) and invites us to enter into His presence through Him and by faith in His blood (Heb. 10:19-23). The Lord Jesus Christ Himself promises to give us whatever we wish when we remain in Him and His words remain in us (John 15:7). Why does He make such a promise? Because when we abide in Him and He in us (John 15:5), whatever we ask is what He is asking through us! In this very real sense it is not us interceding for others at all—but rather, Christ Himself interceding through us.

Thus, it is not a priesthood of people interceding for other people to God, for there is one mediator between man and God, Jesus Christ (1 Tim. 2:5); rather, it is *Christ interceding through us to God* (Rom. 8:34). He inspires our prayers to be in accordance with the Word of God, and that is why He connects His words remaining in us with answering our prayers. All true prayer, therefore, originates with God, flows through us who are in Christ and obeying His commandments, and returns back to God. Such prayers will always be answered, for they are the will of God.

Below are some illustrations of intercessory prayers from the Old and New Testaments. Note that in almost every case the intercessor identifies himself with the sins of his people, names their sins to God and asks God to forgive them. He always appeals to God's character (His mercy, lovingkindness and compassion), to His Name, and to the intercessor's own righteousness before God; the intercessor often asks God to forgive and restore his people for the sake of his own relationship with God. In the same way, we are to pray in Christ (as He is praying in us), interceding for others by naming their sins before God, and asking Him to forgive them for Christ's sake and for our own (John 15:16,17; 16:23,24; 1 John 3:21,22).

What the saints of the Old Testament could only look forward to (the atoning sacrifice of Jesus Christ), we now can look back upon, for the work is finished—and it is for all men (John 19:30; 1 Tim. 2:6). We now know the name of God's mercy: It is Jesus Christ. So whereas the Old Testament saints appealed to God's character (as well as to their own righteous walks with Him) as the reason why He should forgive and restore His people, we have the privilege of appealing to the sufficient work of Christ on the cross and to the excellency of His person, as well as to our position of righteousness in Him and our fellowship with Him.

Just as God answered the prayers of the Old Testament saints by bringing His people to personal and corporate conviction of sin, repentance and restoration, so will He answer our prayers. Because we pray "in Christ," appealing to His work and blood and applying both by faith to those for whom Christ died, we count upon God's enabling and inspiring each to be drawn to Jesus for Himself—both for salvation and revival *through each person's own repentance.*

INTERCESSORY PRAYER: ILLUSTRATIVE EXAMPLES FROM THE OLD AND NEW TESTAMENTS

Nehemiah

When I heard these things, I sat down and wept. For some days I mourned and fasted and prayed before the God of heaven. Then I said:

"O LORD, God of heaven, the great and awesome God, who keeps His covenant of love with those who love Him and obey His commands, let Your ear be attentive and Your eyes open to hear the prayer Your servant is praying before You day and night for Your servants, the people of Israel. *I confess the sins we Israelites, including myself and my father's house, have committed against You. We have acted very wickedly toward You. We have not obeyed the commands, decrees and laws You gave Your servant Moses.*

"Remember the instruction You gave Your servant Moses, saying, 'If you are unfaithful, I will scatter you among the nations, but if you return to Me and obey My commands, then even if your exiled people are at the farthest horizon, I will gather them from there and bring them to the place I have chosen as a dwelling for My Name.'

"They are Your servants and Your people, whom You redeemed by Your great strength and Your mighty hand. O Lord, let Your ear be attentive to the prayer of this Your servant and to the prayer of Your servants who delight in revering Your name. Give Your servant success today by granting him favor in the presence of this man."

I was cupbearer to the king. (Neh. 1:4-11, emphasis added)

Moses

"O LORD, if I have found favor in Your eyes," he said, "then let the Lord go with us. Although this is a stiff-necked people, forgive our wickedness and our sin, and take us as Your inheritance." (Ex. 34:9)

The next day Moses said to the people, "You have committed a great sin. But now I will go up to the LORD; perhaps I can make atonement for your sin." So Moses went back to the LORD and said, *"Oh, what a great sin these people have committed! They have made themselves gods of gold. But now, please forgive their sin—but if not, then blot me out of the book You have written."* (Ex. 32:30-32, emphasis added)

Job

"...My servant Job will pray for you, and I will accept his prayer and not deal with you according to your folly..."...and the Lord accepted Job's prayer. (Job 42:8,9, emphasis added)

Daniel

I prayed to the Lord my God and confessed:

"O Lord, the great and awesome God, who keeps His covenant of love with all who love Him and obey His commands, we have sinned and done wrong. We have been wicked and have rebelled; we have turned away from Your commands and laws. We have not listened to Your servants the prophets, who spoke in Your name to our kings, our princes and our fathers, and to all the people of the land.

"Lord, You are righteous, but this day we are covered with shame—the men of Judah and people of Jerusalem and all Israel, both near and far, in all the countries where You have scattered us because of our unfaithfulness to You. O Lord, we and our kings, our princes and our fathers are covered with shame because we have sinned against You. The Lord our God is merciful and forgiving, even though we

have rebelled against Him; we have not obeyed the LORD our God or kept the laws He gave us through His servants the prophets. All Israel has transgressed Your law and turned away, refusing to obey You.

"Therefore the curses and sworn judgments written in the Law of Moses, the servant of God, have been poured out on us, because we have sinned against You. You have fulfilled the words spoken against us and against our rulers by bringing upon us great disaster. Under the whole heaven nothing has ever been done like what has been done to Jerusalem. Just as it is written in the Law of Moses, all this disaster has come upon us, yet we have not sought the favor of the LORD our God by turning from our sins and giving attention to Your truth. The LORD did not hesitate to bring the disaster upon us, for the LORD our God is righteous in everything He does; yet we have not obeyed Him.

"Now, O Lord our God, who brought Your people out of Egypt with a mighty hand and who made for Yourself a name that endures to this day, we have sinned, we have done wrong. O Lord, in keeping with all Your righteous acts, turn away Your anger and Your wrath from Jerusalem, Your city, Your holy hill. Our sins and the iniquities of our fathers have made Jerusalem and Your people an object of scorn to all those around us.

"Now, our God, hear the prayers and petitions of Your servant. For Your sake, O Lord, look with favor on Your desolate sanctuary. Give ear, O God, and hear; open Your eyes and see the desolation of the city that bears Your Name. We do not make requests of You because we are righteous, but because of Your great mercy. O Lord, listen! O Lord, forgive! O Lord, hear and act! For Your sake, O my God, do not delay, because Your city and Your people bear Your Name."
(Dan. 9:4-19, emphasis added)

Ezra

Then, at the evening sacrifice, I rose from my self-abasement, with my tunic and cloak torn, and fell on my knees with my hands spread out to the LORD my God and prayed:

"O my God, I am too ashamed and disgraced to lift up my face to You, my God, because our sins are higher than our heads and our guilt has reached to the heavens. From the days of our forefathers until now, our guilt has been great. Because of our sins, we and our kings and our priests have been subjected to the sword and captivity, to pillage and humiliation at the hand of foreign kings, as it is to-day...

"What has happened to us is a result of our evil deeds and our great guilt, and yet, our God, You have punished us less than our sins have deserved and have given us a remnant like this. Shall we again break Your commands and intermarry with the peoples who commit such detestable practices? Would You not be angry enough with us to destroy us, leaving us no remnant or survivor? *O Lord, God of Israel, You are righteous! We are left this day as a remnant. Here we are before You in our guilt, though because of it not one of us can stand in Your presence."*

...Then Ezra withdrew from before the house of God and went to the room of Jehohanan son of Eliashib. While he was there, he ate no food and drank no water, because he continued to mourn over the unfaithfulness of the exiles. (Ezra 9:5-7,13-15; 10:6, emphasis added)

Jeremiah

Although our sins testify against us, O Lord, do something for the sake of Your name. For our backsliding is great; we have sinned against You. O Hope of Israel, its Savior in times of distress, why are You like a stranger in the land, like a traveler who stays only a night? Why are You like a man taken by surprise, like a warrior powerless to save?

You are among us, O Lord, and we bear Your name; do not forsake us!...*O Lord, we acknowledge our wickedness and the guilt of our fathers; we have indeed sinned against You. For the sake of Your name do not despise us; do not dishonor Your glorious throne. Remember Your covenant with us and do not break it.* Do any of the worthless idols of the nations bring rain? Do the skies themselves send down showers? No, it is You, O LORD our God. Therefore our hope is in You, for You are the one who does all this. (Jer. 14:7-9,20-22, emphasis added)

Paul

I have great sorrow and unceasing anguish in my heart. For I could wish that I myself were cursed and cut off from Christ for the sake of my brothers, those of my own race, the people of Israel. Theirs is the adoption as sons; theirs the divine glory, the covenants, the receiving of the law, the temple worship and the promises. Theirs are the patriarchs, and from them is traced the human ancestry of Christ, who is God over all, forever praised! Amen

...the Gentiles, who did not pursue righteousness, have obtained it, a righteousness that is by faith; but *Israel, who pursued a law of righteousness, has not attained it. Why not? Because they pursued it not by faith but as if it were by works. They stumbled over the "stumbling stone." As it is written: "See, I lay in Zion a stone that causes men to stumble and a rock that makes them fall, and the one who trusts in Him will never be put to shame."*

Brothers, my heart's desire and prayer to God for the Israelites is that they may be saved. For I can testify about them that they are zealous for God, but their zeal is not based on knowledge. Since they did not know the righteousness that comes from God and sought to establish their own, they did not submit to God's righteousness. Christ is the end of the law so that there may be righteousness for everyone who believes. (Rom. 9:2-5,30-33; 10:1-4, emphasis added)

Stephen

> When they heard this, they were furious and gnashed their teeth at him. But Stephen, full of the Holy Spirit, looked up to heaven and saw the glory of God, and Jesus standing at the right hand of God. "Look," he said, "I see heaven open and the Son of Man standing at the right hand of God." At this they covered their ears and, yelling at the top of their voices, they all rushed at him, dragged him out of the city and began to stone him. Meanwhile, the witnesses laid their clothes at the feet of a young man named Saul. *While they were stoning him, Stephen prayed, "Lord Jesus, receive my spirit." Then he fell on his knees and cried out, "Lord, do not hold this sin against them."* When he had said this, he fell asleep. (Acts 7:54-60, emphasis added)

Jesus

> When they came to the place called the Skull, there they crucified Him, along with the criminals—one on His right, the other on His left. Jesus said, "Father, forgive them, for they do not know what they are doing." (Luke 23:33,34)

COMMANDMENTS OF GOD
THAT CONVICT US OF SIN

This is God's standard, given to mankind in order to convict us of sin:

THE TEN COMMANDMENTS
1. "You shall have no other gods before Me." (Ex. 20:3)
2. "You shall not make for yourself an idol in the form of anything in heaven above or on the earth beneath or in the waters below. You shall not bow down to them or worship them; for I, the LORD your God, am a jealous God, punishing the children for the sin of the fathers to the third and fourth generation of those who hate me, but showing love to a thousand [generations] of those who love Me and keep My commandments." (Ex. 20:4-6)
3. "You shall not misuse the name of the LORD your God, for the Lord will not hold anyone guiltless who misuses His name." (Ex. 20:7)
4. "Remember the Sabbath day by keeping it holy." (Ex. 20:8)
5. "Honor your father and your mother, so that you may live long in the land the Lord your God is giving you." (Ex. 20:12)
6. "You shall not murder." (Ex. 20:13)
7. "You shall not commit adultery." (Ex. 20:14)
8. "You shall not steal." (Ex. 20:15)
9. "You shall not give false testimony against your neighbor." (Ex 20:16)
10. "You shall not covet your neighbor's house. You shall not covet your neighbor's wife...or anything else that belongs to your neighbor." (Ex. 20:17)

THE TWO GREATEST COMMANDMENTS, ACCORDING TO JESUS
"'Love the LORD your God with all your heart and with all your soul and with all your mind.' This is the first and greatest commandment. And the second is like it: 'Love your neighbor as yourself.' All the Law and the Prophets hang on these two commandments." (Matt. 22:37-40)

The Sermon on the Mount (Matt. 5:1-7:29)

The Beatitudes

God will bless the humble, those who mourn, the meek, those who hunger and thirst after righteousness, the merciful, the pure in heart, the peace-makers, those who are persecuted because of righteousness, and those who are insulted and persecuted for Christ's sake. (see Matt. 5:1-11).

Living in This World as Salt and Light

"You are the salt of the earth. But if the salt loses its saltiness, how can it be made salty again? It is no longer good for anything, except to be thrown out and trampled by men. You are the light of the world. A city on a hill cannot be hidden. Neither do people light a lamp and put it under a bowl. Instead they put it on its stand, and it gives light to everyone in the house. In the same way, let your light shine before men, that they may see your good deeds and praise your Father in heaven." (Matt. 5:13–16)

Do not:
1. be angry without cause. (Matt. 5:22)
2. lust in your heart. (Matt. 5:28)
3. divorce your spouse except for marital unfaithfulness. (Matt. 5:31-32)
4. swear. (Matt. 5:34)
5. resist an evil person. (Matt. 5:39)
6. do acts of righteousness before men, to be seen by them. (Matt. 6:1)
7. store up treasure on earth. (Matt. 6:19)
8. worry about your life—what you will eat, drink, or wear. (Matt. 6:25)
9. worry about tomorrow. (Matt. 6:34)
10. judge hypocritically or self-righteously. (Matt. 7:1)
11. give pearls of spiritual teaching to those unable to appreciate them. (Matt. 7:6)

Do:

1. love your enemies and pray for those who persecute you. (Matt. 5:44)
2. be perfect as your Father in heaven is perfect. (Matt. 5:48)
3. pray in private. (Matt. 6:6)
4. forgive others so that your heavenly Father will forgive you. (Matt. 6:14)
5. fast without making it obvious to men that you are fasting. (Matt. 6:17,18)
6. store up treasure in heaven. (Matt. 6:20)
7. seek first His kingdom and righteousness. (Matt. 6:33)
8. ask, seek and knock. (Matt. 7:7)
9. in everything, what you would have others do to you, for this sums up the Law and the Prophets. (Matt. 7:12)
10. enter through the narrow gate. (Matt. 7:13)
11. watch out for false prophets; by their fruit you will recognize them. (Matt. 7:15,16)
12. hear the words of Christ and put them into practice. (Matt. 7:24)

THE GREAT COMMISSION

Then Jesus came to them and said, "All authority in heaven and on earth has been given to Me. Therefore go and make disciples of all nations, baptizing them in the name of the Father and of the Son and of the Holy Spirit, and teaching them to obey everything I have commanded you. And surely I am with you always, to the very end of the age." (Matt. 28:18-20)

LOVING THE LORD AND ONE ANOTHER

"If you obey My commands you will remain in My love, just as I have obeyed my Father's commands and remain in His love...My command is this: Love each other as I have loved you...This is My command: Love each other...As I have loved you, so you must love one another. By this all men will know that you are My disciples, if you love one another." (John 15:10,12,17; 13:34b-35)

CONVICT ME OF MY SINS

Search me, O God, and know my heart; test me and know my anxious thoughts. See if there is any offensive way in me, and lead me in the way everlasting...If we confess our sins, He is faithful and just and will forgive us our sins and purify us from all unrighteousness. (Psa. 139:23,24; 1 John 1:9)

Dear heavenly Father,

Convict me of the terrible sin of not loving You, the Lord, with all my heart, soul, mind and strength. This is the first and greatest commandment. Reveal to me whether I have put anything ahead of You. Enable me to obey Your command to offer my body to You as a living sacrifice, which is my spiritual act of worship. Show me if I have never done this. Show me if, having done so, I have failed to take up my cross every day to follow You.

I belong to You for Your purposes, to approve Your good, pleasing, and perfect will. You saved me from unbelief and rebellion so that I would live in obedience to You through dependence upon the Holy Spirit. May I not be deceived if I have not been doing so! And remind me, too, that I can no longer do the things the world considers valuable, because friendship with the world is hatred of You. (Matt. 22:37; Rom. 12:1,2; 1 Cor. 6:20; 1 Peter 1:18,19; John 15:9,10; Rom. 1:5; 6:5,11-14; James 4:4)

Dear heavenly Father,

I confess that I have not loved others perfectly. Show me when I have been selfish, proud, impatient, unkind, boastful, rude, lazy, fearful, cowardly, angry without cause, a gossip, distrustful, hopeless or unforgiving. Show me when I have thought the worst of someone instead of the best, kept lists of wrongs, lied, stolen, been jealous or envious, or coveted something that belonged to someone else. Forgive me, most of all, for not loving others as I have myself. (1 Cor. 13:4-8; Eph. 4:25-32; Ex. 20:17)

Dear heavenly Father,

Show me whether I have been spending more time, money and energy on physical things than on the pursuit of holiness. I know that there is the constant temptation to devote my attention to what is seen (work, clothes, food, houses, furniture, cars, gardens, vacations, my body, my children, my spouse, sports, etc.) rather than on what is unseen and eternal: Your kingdom. Forgive me for when I have not put Your kingdom first. (Matt. 6:33)

LORD Jesus,

You tell us in the Beatitudes that external righteousness cannot please You, but that You require an inner righteousness. Show me whether I have hated anyone, which is like the sin of murder. Show me whether my thoughts have been impure, which is like the sin of adultery. Reveal to me again that my body is a member of You. Remind me to forgive my enemies, and convict me if I have not done so. Reveal to me, too, that nothing I think or do is hidden from Your sight. (Matt. 5:17,21,22,28; Heb. 4:13; 1 Cor. 6:15,18)

Dear LORD Jesus,

Convict me, too, of any of the following sins: unbelief, disobedience to what I knew would please You, choosing what was okay over what was best, not reading the Bible, not praying, not sharing the gospel, not seeing people without Christ as You see them—lost and without hope, captives of sin and victims of the devil. (Heb. 4:6-9; 2 Cor. 5:18-20; Psa. 119; Isa. 61:1; 1 John 5:19)

Dear heavenly Father,

Show me whether I have hated Your discipline and the trials You provided so that I would grow in faith and give You honor and glory. Remind me that the testing of my faith develops persever-ance and results in maturity. Forgive me for so often wanting to remain childish. And forgive me, too, for complaining and grumbling against You. Enable me to rejoice whenever I face trials because I remember that You discipline me so that I may share in Your holiness. In my struggle against sin I surely have not resisted to the point of shedding blood! (1 Peter 1:6-7; Heb. 12:7-11; James 1:2,4; 1 Cor. 10:10; Heb. 12:4)

Dear heavenly Father,

Show me now, as I pray, whether I have cursed those who hurt me instead of blessing them as I should have. You have commanded me to love my enemies and pray for those who persecute me. You have told me that if I do not forgive others, You will not forgive me. Reveal to me whether I need to go to anyone to ask for forgiveness. Enable me to obey what seems impossible to do! I trust that through Christ I will obey, for in Him I can do all things. (Rom. 12:14; Matt. 5:44; Phil. 4:13)

Precious LORD Jesus,

About my words, Lord, convict me that I am not to curse or use the Lord's name in vain, tear others down with sarcasm or hurtful humor, or be unkind, unforgiving, resentful, bitter, angry, slanderous or malicious. Rather, my words ought to be the result of being under the control of God, the Holy Spirit, expressing God's love and building others up according to their needs. Show me, in the moment of temptation, how to yield to the Holy Spirit, to receive His empowerment to keep from sinning. (James 3:9,10; Ex. 20:7; Eph. 4:29-31; Col. 2:8; Rom. 8:6,14)

Dear heavenly Father,

I also know that it is wrong to be insincere, to be indifferent to evil, to exalt myself over others, to be lukewarm about my faith, to murmur and complain, to grumble when I am afflicted, and to be stingy and inhospitable. (Rom. 12:9-13; Phil. 2:14)

Dear heavenly Father,

Show me, too, that it is a sin to use whatever physical beauty You have given me to tempt others or feed my pride. Convict me that the way I dress ought to be modest, so that I do not tempt others to covet. Reveal to me that You insist on being the Lord of what I wear and that how I dress ought to be for the sake of winning the lost, not for the sake of fitting in with the world or giving me my identity. (1 Cor. 10:31-33; 1 Tim. 2:9)

Precious Father,

Show me whether there is any rebellious way in me, which to You is like the sin of witchcraft. Have I been obedient and respectful to my parents, my husband, my boss, the police, the laws of this nation (including the speed limit), all those in authority, the leaders of my church, my pastor, and so on? Have I been submissive to others in love? Have I loved my wife as myself, considering her needs as important as my own? Have I been proud? (1 Sam. 15:23; Ex. 20:12; 1 Peter 3:7; Rom. 13:1; Heb. 13:17; Eph. 5:21,25-33; James 4:6)

Heavenly Father,

Remind me, if I have looked at sexually explicit or violent images or listened to evil music, that this is sin; I confess it as such and turn away from it. You have commanded me to be holy, to think on whatever is noble, right, pure, lovely, admirable, excellent and praiseworthy. Remind me that if I set my mind on things above, cleansing myself from everything that contaminates body and spirit, I will be an instrument for noble purposes, useful to God and prepared to do any good work. (Gal. 5:19; Phil. 4:8; Col. 3:2; 2 Cor. 7:2; 1 Tim. 2:1)

Dear heavenly Father,

Please do not allow me to be deceived about the sin of robbing You of Your tithes and offerings! May I be someone who claims Your promise that if I bring my whole tithe into my local church that You will throw open the floodgates of heaven and pour out so much blessing that I will not have enough room for it! And remind me, too, that the only debt I should have is the debt of love to my brothers and sisters in Christ. Grant me the grace to store up treasure in heaven and not on this earth, to sow generously, to be a cheerful giver to the LORD Jesus Christ and for His Kingdom's sake. Thank You for Your promise that You will make me rich in every way so that I can be generous on every occasion so that my generosity will result in thanksgiving to God. (Mal. 3:10; Rom. 13:8; Matt. 6:19,20; 2 Cor. 9:6,7,11)

Dear Holy Spirit,

Remind me that prayerlessness is sin. Do fill me with prayer according to the will of the Father and the Son. Enable me to be devoted to prayer, to always lift holy hands in prayer, and to pray without ceasing. Lead me daily to go into my room, to close the door and to pray to God in private. During these times of private prayer, lead me to praise, worship and thank my heavenly Father but also to lift up to Him my family, friends, pastor(s), the leaders of my church, missionaries, other ministries and Christians whom You place on my heart and mind. Help me to be faithful in praying for the lost around me, too, knowing that it is Your will for all men to be saved. Make me faithful and persistent in all kinds of prayer. Give me joy through answered prayer! Enable me to advance Christ's Kingdom through prayer so that great glory may come to Him. (1 Sam. 12:23; Jude 20; Col. 4:2; Titus 2:8; 1 Th. 5:17; Matt 6:6; Heb. 13:15; Eph. 6:18; Titus 2:1-4; Rom. 12:12; Luke 18:1; John 16:24; 1 John 5:14,15)

Dearest Lord Jesus,

Make me a part of fulfilling the Great Commission that I might be used of You to make disciples who obey every one of Your commands. You have given me the Holy Spirit to empower me to be a witness. May I not sin by disobeying His leading and empowerment.

Give me an open door to make known the gospel. Enable me to proclaim it clearly, fearlessly and boldly as I should. Make me wise in the way I act with outsiders; enable me to make the most of every opportunity. May the way I converse with unbelievers be anointed by the Holy Spirit making my conversation with them full of the grace of God and seasoned with wisdom giving me answers to every question they have about You, dear Lord. (Matt. 28:18-20; Acts 1:8; Col. 4:3,4; Eph. 6:19; Acts 4:29; Col 4:5,6)

MY PERSONAL CONFESSION OF SIN

Please take a moment of silence, allowing the Holy Spirit to bring to your mind any sin that you need to confess. Let this be a time for your own confession of specific sins. Remember to receive forgiveness and complete cleansing from God after your confession, according to your faith in God's promise in 1 John 1:9: "If we confess our sins, He is faithful and just and will forgive us our sins and purify us from all unrighteousness."

INTERCEDING FOR THE SINS OF MY FAMILY

Dear heavenly Father,

I come before Your throne of grace to intercede on behalf of my family for our sins. I ask You to convict us, bring us to repentance, forgive us and restore us for Christ's sake. (Please choose from among the following list of sins any for which you need to repent on behalf of your family):

1. Our family did not put You first yesterday (or this week, or for a long time) by having family devotions (Deut. 6:4-7).

2. We did not, as individuals, pray daily for each other, for our church and for the lost around us (Col. 1:10; 4:3; 1 Th. 5:17b; 2 Th. 1:11; James 5:16; 1 Peter 4:7).

3. We haven't shared the gospel (Matt. 28:18-20; Philem. 6).

4. We haven't confessed our sins to each other and to You (Lev. 5:5; 26:40; Psa. 32:5; Acts 19:18; James 5:16).

5. We haven't exhorted one another and helped one another to order our daily lives to bear fruit for Your kingdom (Rom. 12:8; 1 Cor. 14:26; Heb. 10:24).

6. We have not shown by what we have been doing that we love You more than anyone or anything else (James 2:17,24,26).

7. We have kept our personal peace instead of sharing our time, money and lives with others for Your sake (Rom. 12:13; Eph. 4:28; 1 Tim. 6:18; Heb. 13:16).

8. We aren't studying the Bible together or as individuals in other groups (2 Tim. 2:15; Col. 3:16).

9. We have spent too much time on entertainment—TV, sports, shopping, etc. (Matt. 9:37; Eph. 4:12; Col. 3:23; 2 Th. 3:8).

10. We have not kept the Sabbath, which for those who are in Christ is every day, not just Sunday (Col. 2:16; Heb. 4:9-11).

11. We haven't pursued holiness, even though we know that without holiness we shall not see God (2 Tim. 1:9; Titus 1:8; Heb. 12:13,14; 1 Peter 1:15,16; 2 Peter 3:11).

12. We haven't prayed for our nation (1 Tim. 2:1,2).

13. We have grieved You by not trusting Your Word and claiming Your promises (Heb. 11:6).

14. We haven't done all we could to love each other as ourselves; we haven't sympathized with each other (Gal. 5:6b; Heb. 4:15; 1 Peter 1:22; 3:8; 1 John 3:11,18; 4:16,20).

15. Our family is in financial debt, even though You command us to have no debt except the debt of love (Rom. 13:8).

16. Forgive us for every sin of selfishness of heart, tongue and act (1 John 1:9).

17. Please bring to my mind any other specific sin I need to repent of on behalf of my family: _____

Thank You, Father, for hearing my intercession for my family. I ask that You forgive my family because of the blood of Jesus—and that You transform us by the ministry of the Holy Spirit through obedience to Your Word because of Your grace to us in Christ.

For Christ's sake and in His name, Amen

INTERCEDING FOR THE
SINS OF THE CHURCH AT LARGE

Dearest heavenly Father, loving, merciful and full of grace,
We come to You to intercede on behalf of Your church, according
to Your promise to heal our land if we humble ourselves and seek
Your face:

> "...if My people, who are called by My name, will humble
> themselves and pray and seek My face and turn from their
> wicked ways, then will I hear from heaven and will forgive
> their sin and will heal their land." (2 Chr. 7:14)

Father, we come as Your priests, fulfilling the role You have given us,
to intercede for others for what they are not able or willing to
confess for themselves. We join Your Son, the Lord Jesus Christ,
who is at Your right hand and lives forever to intercede for all
believers by His blood, which was shed at Calvary (Rom. 8:34; Heb.
9:21). We believe Your promise that Christ has made forever perfect
those who are being made holy, and we claim that promise for
every born-again believer (Heb. 10:14). We join with Jesus in sympa-
thizing with the weaknesses of our brothers and sisters in Christ
and plead for them as we plead for ourselves and our families (Heb.
4:15,16).

As we intercede for the sins of the body of Your Son, we pray
that You will convict us of these sins, bring us to repentance, forgive
us, and restore us to fellowship, all by Your grace to us in Christ
Jesus, our Lord. We ask solely on the merit of our Savior, because
of His name, His blood, and His work—all because You have loved us
with an everlasting love (Jer. 31:3).

Father, we grieve with You that there is so little "first love" zeal
among those who say they are Yours through Christ (Rev. 2:4). You
saved us for Yourself, to live in Your presence by faith in Jesus, yet
we have filled up our lives with idols of every kind. We agree with
You that we are wretched, pitiful, poor, blind and naked (Rev. 3:17b).

We buy from You, by faith in the blood of Your Son, gold refined in the fire so that we can become rich, white clothes to wear so we can cover our shameful nakedness, and salve to put on our eyes so that we can see (Rev. 3:18).

We grieve with You, Father, Son and Holy Spirit, over all the sins that flow from a lack of love for God: lack of surrender to You; carelessness with the Word of God; disobedience to Your commands; masquerading the strength of the flesh as if it were the Spirit; prayerlessness; hardness of heart; barrenness of life; sexual immorality; perversion of sex, truth, power and authority; greed and covetousness; unbelief; rebellion; worldliness; love of money; idolatry; selfishness; lack of concern for the unsaved; little love for and unity with fellow believers; the selfish use of the gifts of the Spirit; pride and self-exaltation; using the methods of the world to try to achieve Your purposes; divisiveness; stubbornness; tolerating false doctrines; perversion of the true gospel; self-righteousness; self-deception; hypocrisy, and legalism.

We ask that You forgive us for the sake of our precious LORD Jesus. Do not treat us as we deserve but according to Your mercy to us in Him. "Although our sins testify against us, O LORD, do something for the sake of Your name. For our backsliding is great; we have sinned against You" (Jer. 14:7). Enable us to turn to You. Discipline us, that we may share in Your holiness (Heb. 12:19; Rev. 3:19).

According to the new covenant, enable us to live as if guided by the undivided heart You gave us when we were saved; enable us to follow Your decrees and keep Your laws (Ezek. 11:19,20). Enable us to return to You with all our hearts (Jer. 24:7). Inspire us to fear You so that we will not turn away from You any longer (Jer. 32:39-41). "Help us, O God our Savior, for the glory of Your name; deliver us and forgive our sins for Your name's sake" (Psa. 79:9). "You are among us, O Lord, and we bear Your name; do not forsake us!" (Jer. 14:9b).

For the glory of Christ Jesus, Amen

INTERCEDING FOR THE
SINS OF MY LOCAL CHURCH

Confess the sins of your local church and ask God to bring conviction, repentance and restoration.

INTERCEDING FOR THE
SINS OF MY LOCAL CHURCH

PRAYING FOR
BELIEVERS

*And pray in the Spirit on all occasions with all kinds of prayers
and requests. With this in mind, be alert and always keep on
praying for all the saints.*
Ephesians 6:18

PRAYING FOR BELIEVERS

There are nine chapters on praying for believers:

1. *An Overview of God's Will for Believers from New Testament Prayers* – A summary of God's will for believers taken from the prayers recorded in the New Testament.
2. *Prayers from the New Testament for Believers* – New Testament prayers that express God's will for His people.
3. *Prayers Asking God to Accomplish His Will in Believers' Lives* – Prayers asking God to enable us to obey His commandments and to do what is pleasing to Him.
4. *Prayers for Revival* – Prayers asking God to revive His church.
5. *Prayer for Revival of Christian Denominations and Groups* – A comprehensive list of churches and denominations for use in prayer, asking God for revival.
6. *Prayer for Persecuted Believers* – Prayers for believers who are being persecuted in fifty-seven nations of the world.
7. *Names of Believers* – Space for you to list individual believers you're praying for, such as yourself and your family, the members of your extended family, your pastor, the members of your church, your friends, those working in other ministries, and so on.
8. *Personal Prayer Requests* – A place to record personal requests for things such as jobs, health, vacations, safety when traveling, specific guidance, the meeting of your needs, and anything that you would like to ask of God for yourself, your family, and other believers.
9. *Answers to Prayer* – A place to record God's answers and your thanks to Him.

HOW TO USE THIS SECTION

The first chapter summarizes God's will for believers as expressed in New Testament prayers. These pages will enable you to grasp the *scope* of God's will and answer the question "What is God interested in accomplishing in the lives of believers?" Take each Scripture and pray it back to God, asking Him to work it into the lives of believers. This will enable you to pray what God thinks is best for believers.

In the second chapter, *Prayers from the New Testament for Believers*, the verses listed are prayers that can simply be read back to God. (Please note that the verses have only been changed to help you express them as your prayer to God; otherwise they are exactly as they appear in Scripture.) Take one or a few verses each day, and pray that God will accomplish His will in the lives of His people as expressed in the prayer.

Chapter three lists verses expressing God's will for believers. These verses are arranged in groups, with prayers following each group. Take one or more each day, and pray them back to God.

The fourth chapter provides prayers from Scripture asking God to revive His church.

The remaining chapters provide lists to help you pray for Christian denominations, believers by name, persecuted believers throughout the world and your own personal needs. There is also space to record answers to prayer.

Since God the Holy Spirit inspired all of Scripture (2 Tim. 3:16), and since these prayers are based on Scripture, have faith in God's promise:

> This is the confidence we have in approaching God: that if we ask anything according to His will, He hears us. And if we know that He hears us—whatever we ask—we know that we have what we asked of Him. (1 John 5:14,15)

AN OVERVIEW OF GOD'S WILL FOR BELIEVERS FROM NEW TESTAMENT PRAYERS

Dear heavenly Father, may You:

1. Accomplish Your will on earth, as it is in heaven, through us, the body of Your Son. (Matt. 6:10)

2. Give us our daily bread. (Matt. 6:11)

3. Forgive us our sins, as we forgive others who sin against us. (Matt. 6:12)

4. Lead us not into temptation. (Matt. 6:13)

5. Deliver us from the evil one. (Matt. 6:13)

6. Encourage our hearts. (2 Th. 2:17)

7. Strengthen us in every good deed and word. (2 Th. 2:17)

8. Give us the Spirit of wisdom and revelation so that we may know You better. (Eph. 1:17)

9. Enlighten the eyes of our hearts that we may know the hope to which You have called us. (Eph. 1:18)

10. Reveal to us Your glorious inheritance in us. (Eph. 1:18)

11. Reveal to us Your great power to us who believe—the same power that raised Christ from the dead. (Eph. 1:19,20)

12. Fill us with joy, peace and hope by the Holy Spirit. (Rom. 15:13)

13. Make us one with all those who will believe our message; just as You are in the Son and the Son is in You, may they also be in You and Him, so that the world may believe that You have sent Jesus. (John 17:20,21)

14. Bring us to complete unity to let the world know You sent Jesus and that You love us as You love Him. (John 17:23)

15. Give us endurance, encouragement and unity as we follow Christ, so that with one heart and mouth we may glorify You. (Rom. 15:5,6)

16. Protect us by the power of Christ's name so that we may be one as You and He are one. (John 17:11)

17. Give us peace at all times and in every way. (2 Th. 3:16)

18. Enable us to enjoy good health, and enable all to go well with us. (3 John 2)

19. Enable us to be active in sharing our faith so that we will know every good thing we have in Christ. (Phm. 6)

20. Fill us with the knowledge of Your will through spiritual wisdom and understanding, so that we may live lives worthy of You and please You in every way. (Col. 1:9,10)

21. Sanctify us through and through. Make us blameless—spirit, soul and body—for Christ's coming; You are faithful and will do it. (1 Th. 5:23,24)

22. Sanctify us by the truth; Your Word is truth. (John 17:17)

23. Direct our hearts into Your love and Christ's perseverance. (2 Th. 3:5)

24. Enable our love to abound in knowledge and insight so that we may discern what is best, in order to be pure and blameless when Christ returns—filled with the fruit of righteousness that comes through Him, for Your glory and praise. (Phil. 1:9-11)

25. Make our love increase and overflow for each other and everyone else, just as it does for You. (1 Th. 3:12)

26. Strengthen our hearts so that we will be blameless and holy in Your presence when Christ comes. (1 Th. 3:13)

27. Count us worthy of Your calling. (2 Th. 1:11)

28. By Your power, fulfill every good purpose of ours and every act prompted by faith. (2 Th. 1:11)

29. Equip us with everything good for doing Your will; work in us what is pleasing to You. (Heb. 13:21)

30. Present us before Your presence without fault and with great joy. (Jude 24)

31. Rescue us from unbelievers and make our service acceptable to the saints. (Rom. 15:31)

32. Establish us by Your gospel and by the proclamation of Christ. (Rom. 16:25)

33. Strengthen us with power through the Holy Spirit in our inner beings so that Christ may dwell in us. (Eph. 3:17)

34. Give us power to grasp how wide, long, high and deep is Your love for us in Christ, so that we may be filled with You. (Eph. 3:18)

35. Do immeasurably more than all we ask or imagine. (Eph. 3:20)

36. Protect us from the evil one. (John 17:15)

37. Give us words when we open our mouths to share the gospel; enable us to declare it fearlessly as we should. (Eph. 6:19,20)

38. Enable us to speak Your Word with great boldness. (Acts 4:29)

39. Enable us to pray as Stephen did when he was stoned to death. (Acts 7:60)

40. Enable us to forgive those who abuse us, even as our Lord forgave those who crucified Him. (Luke 23:34)

41. Spread the message of the Lord rapidly and cause it to be honored. Deliver us from wicked and evil men who don't have faith. Strengthen and protect us from the Evil One. (2 Th. 3:1-3)

42. Give us the grace of the LORD Jesus Christ, the love of God, and the fellowship of the Holy Spirit. (2 Cor. 13:14)

PRAYERS FROM THE
NEW TESTAMENT FOR BELIEVERS

(These prayers are from the NIV and are paraphrased by the author)

"'Our Father in heaven, hallowed be Your name, Your kingdom come, Your will be done on earth as it is in heaven. Give us today our daily bread. Forgive us our debts, as we also have forgiven our debtors. And lead us not into temptation, but deliver us from the evil one.'" (Matt. 6:9-13)

Dear heavenly Father,
May our LORD Jesus Christ Himself and You, our Father, who loved us and by Your grace gave us eternal encouragement and good hope, encourage our hearts and strengthen us in every good deed and word. (2 Th. 2:16,17)

Dear heavenly Father,
I ask that You, the God of our LORD Jesus Christ, the glorious Father, give us the Spirit of wisdom and revelation, so that we may know You better. I pray also that the eyes of our hearts may be enlightened in order that we may know the hope to which You have called us, the riches of Your glorious inheritance in the saints, and Your incomparably great power for us who believe. That power is like the working of Your mighty strength, which You exerted in Christ when You raised Him from the dead and seated Him at Your right hand in the heavenly realms. (Eph. 1:17-20)

Dear heavenly Father,
May You, the God of hope, fill us with all joy and peace as we trust in You, so that we may overflow with hope by the power of the Holy Spirit. (Rom. 15:13)

101

Dear heavenly Father,

Make us one with all those who will believe our message; just as You are in the Son and the Son is in You, may they also be in You and Him, so that the world may believe that You have sent Jesus. (John 17:20,21)

Dear heavenly Father,

May we be brought to complete unity to let the world know that You sent Jesus and have loved us even as You have loved Him. (John 17:23)

Dear heavenly Father,

May You, the God who gives endurance and encouragement, give us a spirit of unity among ourselves as we follow Christ Jesus, so that with one heart and mouth we may glorify You, the God and Father of our Lord Jesus Christ. (Rom. 15:5,6)

Dear holy Father,

Protect us by the power of Your name—the name You gave Jesus—so that we who believe may be one as You and He are one. (John 17:11)

Dear Lord Jesus,

May You, the LORD of peace, give us peace at all times and in every way. May You be with us all. (2 Th. 3:16)

Dear heavenly Father,

I pray that we may enjoy good health and that all may go well with us, even as our souls are getting along well. (3 John 2)

Dear heavenly Father,
I pray that we may be active in sharing our faith, so that we will have a full understanding of every good thing we have in Christ. (Phm. 6)

Dear heavenly Father,
Since the gospel is bearing fruit and growing among us since the day we heard it and understood God's grace, we pray that You will fill us with the knowledge of Your will through all spiritual wisdom and understanding, in order that we may live lives worthy of the Lord and please You in every way. (Col. 1:6,9,10)

Dear holy Father,
May You, the God of peace, sanctify us through and through. May we be kept blameless—spirit, soul, and body—at the coming of our LORD Jesus Christ. You who have called us are faithful and will do it. (1 Th. 5:23,24)

Dear Father,
Sanctify us by the truth; Your Word is truth. (John 17:17)

Dear heavenly Father,
May the Lord direct our hearts into God's love and Christ's perse-verance. (2 Th. 3:5)

Dear heavenly Father,
This is my prayer: that our love may abound more and more in knowledge and depth of insight, so that we may be able to discern what is best and be pure and blameless until the day of Christ, filled with the fruit of righteousness that comes through Jesus Christ—to the glory and praise of God. (Phil. 1:9-11)

Dear heavenly Father,

I pray that You will make our love increase and overflow for each other and for everyone else, just as it does for You. May You strengthen our hearts so that we will be blameless and holy in Your presence when our Lord Jesus comes with all His holy ones. (1 Th. 3:12,13)

Dear heavenly Father,

I pray that You may count us worthy of Your calling, and that by Your power You may fulfill every good purpose of ours and every act prompted by our faith. (2 Th. 1:11)

Dear heavenly Father,

May You, the God of peace, who through the blood of the eternal covenant brought back from the dead our LORD Jesus, that great Shepherd of the sheep, equip us with everything good for doing Your will; may You also work in us what is pleasing to You, through Jesus Christ, to whom be glory for ever and ever. Amen (Heb. 13:20,21)

Dear heavenly Father,

Please keep us from falling and present us before Your glorious presence without fault and with great joy. For You are the only God, our Savior; to You be glory, majesty, power, and authority through Jesus Christ our Lord, before all ages, now and forevermore! Amen (Jude 24,25)

Dear heavenly Father,

We pray that we may be rescued from the unbelievers in our "Judea" and that our service in our "Jerusalem" may be acceptable to the saints there. (Rom. 15:31)

Dear heavenly Father,

Establish us by the gospel and the proclamation of Jesus Christ, according to the revelation of the mystery hidden for long ages past, but now revealed and made known through the prophetic writings by Your command, eternal God, so that all nations might believe and obey Him. To You, the only wise God, be glory forever through Jesus Christ! Amen (Rom. 16:25)

Dear heavenly Father,

We pray that out of Your glorious riches You may strengthen us with power through Your Spirit in our inner being, so that Christ may dwell in our hearts through faith. And we pray that we, being rooted and established in love, may have power, together with all the saints, to grasp how wide and long and high and deep is the love of Christ and to know this love that surpasses knowledge—that we may be filled to the measure of all the fullness of God. (Eph. 3:16-19)

Dear heavenly Father,

We pray that You will do immeasurably more than all we ask or imagine, according to Your power that is at work within us; to You be glory in the church and in Christ Jesus throughout all generations, for ever and ever! Amen (Eph. 3:20,21)

Dear heavenly Father,

Our prayer is not that You take us out of the world, but that You protect us from the evil one. (John 17:15)

Dear heavenly Father,

We pray also for us, that whenever we open our mouths, words may be given us so that we will fearlessly make known the mystery of the gospel. (Eph. 6:19)

Dear heavenly Father,
Enable Your servants to speak Your Word with great boldness. (Acts 4:29)

Dear heavenly Father,
Enable us to cry out to You for the sake of the gospel as Stephen did when he was being stoned. He cried out, "Lord, do not hold this sin against them." (Acts 7:60)

Dear heavenly Father,
Enable us to pray for those who abuse us and persecute us for the sake of the gospel—even as Jesus prayed, "Father, forgive them, for they do not know what they are doing." (Luke 23:34)

Dear heavenly Father,
We pray that the message of the Lord may spread rapidly and be honored as it was with the early church. Deliver us from wicked and evil men, for not everyone has faith. Strengthen and protect us from the evil one. (2 Th. 3:1-3)

Dear heavenly Father,
May the grace of the LORD Jesus Christ, and the love of God, and the fellowship of the Holy Spirit be with us all. (2 Cor. 13:14)

PRAYERS ASKING GOD TO ACCOMPLISH HIS WILL IN BELIEVERS' LIVES

Dear heavenly Father,

Because only You are good (Matt. 19:17) and because it is only by Your grace that we can become people who are like Your Son (Eph. 2:10; 2 Cor. 3:18), we pray for all believers, that You enable us to be:

Merciful

"It is not the healthy who need a doctor, but the sick. But go and learn what this means: 'I desire *mercy*, not sacrifice.' For I have not come to call the righteous, but sinners." (Matt. 9:12,13, emphasis added)

because judgment without *mercy* will be shown to anyone who has not been merciful. Mercy triumphs over judgment! (James 2:13, emphasis added)

Dear heavenly Father,

By Your Spirit, spread in our hearts an understanding of the mercy You have shown us who were sinners saved by Your grace. Enable us to have that same attitude of mercy to others—both believers and unbelievers. May Your mercy in us triumph over our natural inclination to judge others!

In Your mercy, which is in Christ, Amen

Faithful

"According to your *faith* will it be done to you" (Matt. 9:29, emphasis added)

"I tell you the truth, if you have *faith* as small as a mustard seed, you can say to this mountain, 'Move from here to there' and it will move. Nothing will be impossible for you." (Matt. 17:20, emphasis added)

"If you *believe*, you will receive whatever you ask for in prayer." (Matt. 21:22, emphasis added)

For in the gospel a righteousness from God is revealed, a righteousness that is by *faith* from first to last, just as it is written: "The righteous will live by *faith*." (Rom. 1:17, emphasis added)

And everything that does not come from *faith* is sin. (Rom. 14:23, emphasis added)

A man is not justified by observing the law, but by *faith* in Jesus Christ. So we, too, have put our *faith* in Christ Jesus that we may be justified by *faith* in Christ and not by observing the law, because by observing the law no one will be justified. (Gal. 2:16, emphasis added)

And without *faith* it is impossible to please God, because anyone who comes to Him must believe that He exists and that He rewards those who earnestly seek Him. (Heb. 11:6, emphasis added)

> Dear heavenly Father,
> Enable us to be people of faith—faith in Christ as we begin our walk with You when we receive Him as our Savior, but also faith that grows as we daily believe in Him to set us apart for Your purposes. Only You can transform us. Enable us to trust that You will. Make us a people who live by faith. Reward all those who earnestly seek You!
>
> For Christ's sake, Amen

Loving

"'*Love* the LORD your God with all your heart and with all your soul and with all your mind.' This is the first and greatest commandment. And the second is like it: '*Love* your neighbor as yourself.' All the Law and the Prophets hang on these two commandments." (Matt. 22:37-40, emphasis added)

"A new command I give you: *Love* one another. As I have loved you, so you must *love* one another. By this all men will know that you are My disciples, if you *love* one another." (John 13:34,35, emphasis added)

And now these three remain: faith, hope and *love*. But the greatest of these is *love*. (1 Cor. 13:13, emphasis added)

The only thing that counts is faith expressing itself through *love*. (Gal. 5:6b, emphasis added)

Be imitators of God, therefore, as dearly *loved* children and live a life of *love*, just as Christ *loved* us and gave Himself up for us as a fragrant offering and sacrifice to God. (Eph. 5:1,2, emphasis added)

> Dear heavenly Father,
> We pray that You will shed Your love abroad in our hearts by Your Spirit, so that we will have great love for You and for one another. We count on You to give us Your love through Christ Jesus, the LORD.
>
> In Him who is love, Jesus, Amen

Consecrated

"Anyone who loves his father or mother more than Me is not worthy of Me; anyone who loves his son or daughter more than Me is not worthy of Me; and *anyone who does not take his cross and follow Me is not worthy of Me*. Whoever finds his life will lose it, and whoever loses his life for My sake will find it." (Matt. 10:37-39, emphasis added)

Therefore, I urge you, brothers, in view of God's mercy, to *offer your bodies as living sacrifices*, holy and pleasing to God—this is your spiritual act of worship. Do not conform any longer to the pattern of this world, but be transformed by the renewing of your mind. Then you will be able to test and approve what God's will is—His good, pleasing and perfect will. (Rom. 12:1,2, emphasis added)

Who have been chosen according to the foreknowledge of God the Father, through the sanctifying work of the Spirit, *for obedience to Jesus Christ* and sprinkling by His blood...(1 Peter 1:2, emphasis added)

> Dear heavenly Father,
> Convict all of us who believe in Christ of our need to give ourselves up to You, irrevocably, as living sacrifices, to live for Your good pleasure, not our own. Your command in this regard is quite clear. We have been saved for Your purposes and for Your

glory. It is written, "And He died for all, that those who live should no longer live for themselves but for Him who died for them and was raised again" (2 Cor 5:15). May this be true for all who call themselves Christians because of Your grace, Your empowerment and Your discipline.

For the glory of God, Amen

Worthy of Christ

"Anyone who loves his father or mother more than Me is not *worthy* of Me; anyone who loves his son or daughter more than Me is not *worthy* of Me; and anyone who does not take his cross and follow Me is not *worthy* of Me." (Matt. 10:37,38, emphasis added)

And we pray this in order that you may live a life *worthy* of the Lord and may please Him in every way: bearing fruit in every good work, growing in the knowledge of God. (Col. 1:10, emphasis added)

As a prisoner for the Lord, then, I urge you to live a life *worthy* of the calling you have received. (Eph. 4:1, emphasis added)

Dear heavenly Father,
Enable us who believe in Christ to put Him first in our lives, ahead of everyone else, even our children and ourselves. And work in us what is pleasing to You, so that we may live a life worthy of the Lord.

For the glory of Christ, Amen

Prayerful

Do not be anxious about anything, but in everything, by *prayer* and petition, with thanksgiving, present your requests to God. And the peace of God, which transcends all understanding, will guard your hearts and your minds in Christ Jesus. (Phil. 4:6,7, emphasis added)

Devote yourselves to *prayer*, being watchful and thankful. (Col. 4:2, emphasis added)

And *pray* in the Spirit on all occasions with all kinds of *prayers* and requests. With this in mind, be alert and always keep on *praying* for all the saints. (Eph. 6:18, emphasis added)

pray continually... (1 Th. 5:17, emphasis added)

"But I tell you: Love your enemies and *pray* for those who persecute you, that you may be sons of your Father in heaven. He causes His sun to rise on the evil and the good, and sends rain on the righteous and the unrighteous." (Matt. 5:44,45, emphasis added)

The end of all things is near. Therefore be clear minded and self-controlled so that you can *pray*. (1 Peter 4:7, emphasis added)

Dear heavenly Father,
Remind us to pray at all times, to be watchful, thankful, alert, clear minded and self-controlled. By Your Spirit, enable us to pray for all the saints and for everything in our lives according to Your will and for Your glory.
In our peace, the Lord Jesus, Amen

Fruitful

"I am the vine; you are the branches. If a man remains in Me and I in him, he will bear much *fruit*; apart from Me you can do nothing." (John 15:5, emphasis added)

"But the seed on good soil stands for those with a noble and good heart, who hear the word, retain it, and by persevering *produce a crop.*" (Luke 8:15, emphasis added)

And we pray this in order that you may live a life worthy of the Lord and may please Him in every way: *bearing fruit* in every good work,…(Col. 1:10, emphasis added)

And this is my prayer: that your love may abound more and more in knowledge and depth of insight, so that you may be able to discern what is best and may be pure and blameless until the day of Christ, filled with the *fruit of righteousness* that comes through Jesus Christ—to the glory and praise of God. (Phil. 1:9-11, emphasis added)

But the *fruit of the Spirit* is love, joy, peace, patience, kindness, goodness, faithfulness, gentleness and self-control. Against such things there is no law. (Gal. 5:22,23, emphasis added)

> Dear heavenly Father,
> It is Your will that we bear fruit by abiding in Christ, with noble and good hearts, with abounding love that is insightful, with discernment, and with faith that we are no longer under law, but under the blessed ministry of the Holy Spirit. Enable all believers to be fruitful—by Your grace and for Your glory.
>
> For the sake of the Lord, Amen

Devoted

"No one can serve two masters. Either he will hate the one and love the other, or he will be *devoted* to the one and despise the other. You cannot serve both God and Money." (Matt. 6:24, emphasis added)

They *devoted* themselves to the apostles' teaching and to the fellowship, to the breaking of bread and to prayer. (Acts 2:42, emphasis added)

Be *devoted* to one another in brotherly love. Honor one another above yourselves. (Rom. 12:10, emphasis added)

"Yet if you *devote* your heart to Him and stretch out your hands to Him, if you put away the sin that is in your hand and allow no evil to dwell in your tent, then you will lift up your face without shame; you will stand firm and without fear." (Job 11:13-15, emphasis added)

Guard my life, for I am *devoted* to you. You are my God; save your servant who trusts in you. (Psa. 86:2, emphasis added)

> Dear heavenly Father,
> Convict us of the devotion that You require of all who call upon the name of the Lord. Enable us to be devoted to You, to the Bible, to fellowship, to prayer and to one another. Guard us and enable us to stand firm as we trust in You and devote ourselves to You.
>
> Amen

Forgiving

"*Forgive* us our debts, as we also have *forgiven* our debtors. For if you *forgive* men when they sin against you, your heavenly Father will also *forgive* you. But if you do not *forgive* men their sins, your Father will not *forgive* your sins." (Matt. 6:12,14,15, emphasis added)

"Then the master called the servant in. 'You wicked servant,' he said, 'I canceled all that debt of yours because you begged me to. Shouldn't you have had mercy on your fellow servant just as I had on you?' In anger his master turned him over to the jailers to be tortured, until he should pay back all he owed. This is how My heavenly Father will treat each of you unless you *forgive* your brother from your heart." (Matt. 18:32-35, emphasis added)

"And when you stand praying, if you hold anything against anyone, *forgive* him, so that your Father in heaven may *forgive* you your sins." (Mark 11:25, emphasis added)

"Do not judge, and you will not be judged. Do not condemn, and you will not be condemned. *Forgive*, and you will be *forgiven.*" (Luke 6:37, emphasis added)

> Dear heavenly Father,
> How hard it is to forgive from the heart! Who can do it without Your grace? No one. Enable us to do what is impossible, so that we, too, may be forgiven. And reveal to us that when we forgive others, we help to set them free—even as we were set free by You.
> In the One who has given us forgiveness, Amen

Full of Grace

From the fullness of His *grace* we have all received one blessing after another. For the law was given through Moses; *grace* and truth came through Jesus Christ. (John 1:16,17, emphasis added)

For it is by *grace* you have been saved, through faith—and this not from yourselves, it is the gift of God—not by works, so that no one can boast. (Eph. 2:8,9, emphasis added)

113

There is one body and one Spirit—just as you were called to one hope when you were called—one Lord, one faith, one baptism; one God and Father of all, who is over all and through all and in all. But to each one of us *grace* has been given as Christ apportioned it. (Eph. 4:4-7, emphasis added)

But by the *grace* of God I am what I am, and His *grace* to me was not without effect. No, I worked harder than all of them—yet not I, but the *grace* of God that was with me. (1 Cor. 15:10, emphasis added)

> Dear heavenly Father,
>
> Enable us to comprehend the marvelous grace You have poured out upon all of us who believe. You saved us not because we had any worthiness, but simply out of Your love and kindness. May we never boast that we were saved by our own self-effort. And may we, like the apostle Paul, become all that Your grace enables us to be.
>
> Amen

Obedient

Through Him and for His name's sake, we received grace and apostleship to call people from among all the Gentiles to the *obedience* that comes from faith. (Rom. 1:5, emphasis added)

The Lord commanded us to *obey* all these decrees and to fear the LORD our God, so that we might always prosper and be kept alive, as is the case today. (Deut. 6:24, emphasis added)

Who have been chosen according to the foreknowledge of God the Father, through the sanctifying work of the Spirit, for *obedience* to Jesus Christ and sprinkling by His blood: Grace and peace be yours in abundance. (1 Peter 1:2, emphasis added)

Obey your leaders and submit to their authority...Children, *obey* your parents in the Lord,...(Heb. 13:17; Eph. 6:1, emphasis added)

"If anyone loves Me, he will *obey* My teaching...He who does not love Me will not *obey* My teaching..." (John 14:23,24, emphasis added)

Those who *obey* His commands live in Him, and He in them...(1 John 3:24, emphasis added)

> Dear heavenly Father,
>
> Inspire believers to obey all Your commands and to be undeceived about the necessity of obedience. You have always required obedience; You require it still. We who have the Holy Spirit are willing and able to obey!
>
> In Christ, our obedience, Amen

Pure

I am jealous for you with a godly jealousy. I promised you to one husband, to Christ, so that I might present you as a *pure* virgin to Him. But I am afraid that just as Eve was deceived by the serpent's cunning, your minds may somehow be led astray from your sincere and *pure* devotion to Christ. (2 Cor. 11:2,3, emphasis added)

Everyone who has this hope in him purifies himself, just as He is *pure*. (1 John 3:3, emphasis added)

Since we have these promises, dear friends, let us *purify* ourselves from everything that contaminates body and spirit, perfecting holiness out of reverence for God. (2 Cor. 7:1, emphasis added)

"Blessed are the *pure* in heart, for they will see God." (Matt. 5:8, emphasis added)

Marriage should be honored by all, and the marriage bed kept *pure*, for God will judge the adulterer and all the sexually immoral. (Heb. 13:4, emphasis added)

> Dear heavenly Father,
>
> How can we be pure unless You keep us close to You? We ask You to purify our hearts and our lives so that we will see You. Protect our marriages from sexual temptation and immorality; may we not be deceived in this regard! Protect us, also, from the temptation of the devil, who seeks to lead us astray from our devotion to the Lord. Remind us of the hope that is certain and of the promises of God,

so that we will purify ourselves from everything that would contaminate our bodies and spirits. Enable us to perfect holiness out of reverence for You.

For the Lord's sake, Amen

Servants

Fear the LORD your God, *serve* Him only…(Deut. 6:13, emphasis added)

"Not so with you. Instead, whoever wants to become great among you must be your *servant,* and whoever wants to be first must be your slave—just as the Son of Man *did not come to be served, but to serve,* and to give His life as a ransom for many." (Matt. 20:26-28, emphasis added)

You, my brothers, were called to be free. But do not use your freedom to indulge the sinful nature; rather, *serve* one another in love. The entire law is summed up in a single command: "Love your neighbor as yourself." (Gal. 5:13,14, emphasis added)

Each one should use whatever gift he has received to *serve* others, faithfully administering God's grace in its various forms. If anyone speaks, he should do it as one speaking the very words of God. If anyone *serves,* he should do it with the strength God provides,…(1 Peter 4:10,11, emphasis added)

What, after all, is Apollos? And what is Paul? Only *servants,* through whom you came to believe—as the Lord has assigned to each his task. I planted the seed, Apollos watered it, but God made it grow. So neither he who plants nor he who waters is anything, but only God, who makes things grow. (1 Cor. 3:5-7, emphasis added)

Dear heavenly Father,

Enlighten us so that we may grasp this concept of servanthood—that we are here to serve You only—and one another with the grace and strength You provide. Remind us that everything we have, everything we are, and everything we do is from You and for You.

Because of the Man of Grace, Jesus, Amen

Good Stewards

"'For everyone who has will be given more, and he will have an abundance. Whoever does not have, even what he has will be taken from him.'" (Matt. 25:29)

We have different gifts, according to the grace given us...It was He who gave some to be apostles, some to be prophets, some to be evangelists, and some to be pastors and teachers, to prepare God's people for works of service, so that the body of Christ may be built up until we all reach unity in the faith and in the knowledge of the Son of God...(Rom. 12:6; Eph. 4:11-13)

And God is able to make all grace abound to you, so that in all things at all times, having all that you need, you will abound in every good work. (2 Cor. 9:8)

> Dear heavenly Father,
> Enable us to be good stewards of the grace and gifts You have given us, so that we will glorify You as we each do our part. Only together can we become mature, attaining the whole measure of the fullness of Christ.
> For Christ's sake and glory, Amen

Lovers of the Truth

"If you hold to My teaching, you are really My disciples. Then you will know the *truth*, and the *truth* will set you free." (John 8:31,32, emphasis added)

"But when He, the Spirit of *truth*, comes, He will guide you into all *truth*..." (John 16:13, emphasis added)

"Sanctify them by the *truth*; Your word is *truth*." (John 17:17, emphasis added)

And the Word was God. The Word became flesh and made His dwelling among us...(John 1:1,14)

Jesus answered, "I am the way and the *truth* and the life. No one comes to the Father except through Me." (John 14:6, emphasis added)

The coming of the lawless one will be in accordance with the work of Satan displayed in all kinds of counterfeit miracles, signs and wonders, and in every sort of evil that deceives those who are perishing. They perish because they refused to *love the truth* and so be saved. (2 Th. 2:9,10, emphasis added)

> Dear heavenly Father,
> Convict us that Your Word is the truth—and Christ is the Word! He is the truth who sets us free—and He reveals Himself only to those who hold to His teaching. By Your grace, may we love the truth, who is Christ. May we never be deceived into thinking that the Word of God is not the only way to the Father! Sanctify us through the ministry of the Holy Spirit through the written Word, that we may be filled with Jesus.
>
> In the Word of God, Amen

Noble

In a large house there are articles not only of gold and silver, but also of wood and clay; some are for *noble* purposes and some for ignoble. If a man cleanses himself from the latter, he will be an instrument for *noble* purposes, made holy, useful to the Master and prepared to do any good work. (2 Tim. 2:20,21, emphasis added)

Finally, brothers, whatever is true, whatever is *noble*, whatever is right, whatever is pure, whatever is lovely, whatever is admirable—if anything is excellent or praiseworthy—think about such things. (Phil. 4:8, emphasis added)

But the seed on good soil stands for those with a *noble* and good heart, who hear the word, retain it, and by persevering produce a crop. (Luke 8:15, emphasis added)

Now the Bereans were of more *noble* character than the Thessalonians, for they received the message with great eagerness and examined the Scriptures every day to see if what Paul said was true. (Acts 17:11, emphasis added)

Dear heavenly Father,

May we be noble-minded and noble-hearted people, who respond to Your grace with perseverance, proving ourselves to be useful to You and prepared to do any good work. And may we test all things by the Scriptures, reverencing them as the judge of all truth and submitting to their authority in all matters of life and godliness.

For the sake of our Lord, Amen

Prayers for Revival

Revival is defined as what occurs when God pours out His Holy Spirit upon His people. This pouring out of the Holy Spirit results characteristically in the following: a seeking after the Lord in much prayer and with wholeheartedness; the anointing of preachers with power and courage resulting in the ability to preach the gospel with great boldness; the salvation of many; devotion to the Scriptures, to the fellowship of the Body, and to the ordinances of the church; love, unity, generosity, and holy living; the fear of the Lord, awe, adoration, and praise; confession of sin and repentance from it; the removal of evil things; obedience to the word of God; and the spreading of the word of the Lord in power.

Instances of revival in the Bible are: under Joshua (Josh. 5:2-9), Samuel (I Sam. 7:1-6), Elijah (1 Kings 18:17-14), Jehoash and Jehoiada (2 Kings 11-12; 2 Chr. 23,24), Hezekiah (2 Kings 18:1-7; 2 Chr. 29:31), Josiah (2 Kings 22,23; 2 Chr. 34,35), Asa (2 Chr. 14:2-5; 15:1-14), Manasseh (2 Chr. 33:12-19), in Ninevah (John 3:4-10), at Pentecost and post-Pentecostal times (Acts 2:1-42,46-47; 4:4; 5:14; 6:7; 9:35; 11:20,21; 12:24; 14:1; 19:17-20).

In the Old as well as the New Testaments, and in the history of the Church, the pouring out of the Holy Spirit is often brought about through heartfelt prayer and often, fasting. As you pray for revival on the following pages, remember that revival pleases God for it inspires and empowers us to return to our first love of Christ and results in many others being saved as well.

Dear heavenly Father,

We come before Your throne to beseech You for revival. We pray according to the Scripture You have inspired and given to us, and we plead for mercy and grace according to Your will, secured for us by Jesus Christ, our Savior and Lord:

Do not hold against us the sins of the fathers; may Your mercy come quickly to meet us, for we are in desperate need. Help us, O God our Savior, for the glory of Your name; deliver us and forgive our sins for Your name's sake. (Psa. 79:8,9)

Restore us, O God; make Your face shine upon us, that we may be saved – Restore us, O God Almighty; make Your face shine upon us, that we may be saved – Then we will not turn away from You; revive us, and we will call on Your name. Restore us, O LORD God Almighty; make Your face shine upon us, that we may be saved. (Psa. 80:3,7,18,19)

Teach me Your way, O LORD, and I will walk in Your truth; give me an undivided heart, that I may fear Your name. I will praise You, O Lord my God, with all my heart; I will glorify Your name forever. (Psa. 86:11,12)

Although our sins testify against us, O LORD, do something for the sake of Your name. For our backsliding is great; we have sinned against You – You are among us, O LORD, and we bear Your name; do not forsake us! (Jer. 14:7,9b)

Heal me, O LORD, and I will be healed; save me and I will be saved, for You are the one I praise. (Jer. 17:14)

O LORD, we acknowledge our wickedness and the guilt of our fathers; we have indeed sinned against You. For the sake of Your name do not despise us; do not dishonor Your glorious throne. Remember Your covenant with us and do not break it. Do any of the worthless idols of the nations bring rain? Do the skies themselves send down showers? No, it is You, O LORD our God. Therefore our hope is in You, for You are the one who does all this. (Jer. 14:20-22)

Dear heavenly Father,
We ask You to do what You have promised – to put in us what You ask of us and to revive us for the sake of the sufficiency of the blood, work, and person of the Lord Jesus Christ:

"I will give them singleness of heart and action, so that they will always fear Me for their own good and the good of their children after them. I will make an everlasting covenant with them: I will never stop doing good to them, and I will inspire them to fear Me, so that they will never turn away from Me. I will rejoice in doing them good and will assuredly plant them in this land with all my heart and soul." (Jer. 32:39-41)

"I will give them an undivided heart and put a new spirit in them; I will remove from them their heart of stone and give them a heart of flesh. Then they will follow My decrees and be careful to keep My laws. They will be My people, and I will be their God." (Ezek. 11:19,20)

"For I know the plans I have for you," declares the LORD, "plans to prosper you and not to harm you, plans to give you hope and a future. Then you will call upon Me and come and pray to Me, and I will listen to you. You will seek Me and find Me when you seek Me with all your heart." (Jer. 29:11-13)

"The time is coming, declares the Lord, when I will make a new covenant with the house of Israel and with the house of Judah. It will not be like the covenant I made with their forefathers when I took them by the hand to lead them out of Egypt, because they did not remain faithful to My covenant, and I turned away from them, declares the Lord. This is the covenant I will make with the house of Israel after that time, declares the Lord. I will put My laws in their minds and write them on their hearts. I will be their God, and they will be My people. No longer will a man teach his neighbor, or a man his brother, saying, 'Know the Lord,' because they will all know Me, from the least of them to the greatest. For I will forgive their wickedness and will remember their sins no more." (Heb. 8:8-12)

The Holy Spirit also testifies to us about this. First He says: "This is the covenant I will make with them after that time, says the Lord. I will put My laws in their hearts, and I will write them on their minds." Then He adds: "Their sins and lawless acts I will remember no more." And where these have been forgiven, there is no longer any sacrifice for sin. (Heb. 10:15-18)

Dearest Father in heaven—almighty, just, sovereign and exceedingly merciful Lord,

We come to You in prayer, with hearts profoundly burdened with the desire that You once again revive us, causing us who say we believe in Your wonderful Son, Jesus, to love Him and You with all our hearts, souls, minds and strength (Matt. 22:37). We ask You to pour out Your Spirit—the Spirit of holiness, truth, and of Christ—that we may realize the unity of His body, which will be the greatest witness of all that You have given Him as Savior of this wicked, perishing world (Rom. 1:4; John 14:17; 2 Cor. 3:17; John 17:21).

We believe that You are a God of mercy and that the name of Your mercy is Christ (Psa. 25:6; Eph. 2:4; 1 Peter 1:3). In Him, You have already fulfilled the just demands of Your wrath against the sin and ungodliness of all humanity, once and for all at the cross (Rom. 3:26; 5:9; Col. 1:20,22). We look to the cross, to the crucified body of our precious Savior, and to His shed blood as the only reason why You should answer our prayer (Heb. 10:19-22).

We humbly acknowledge that although we seek to walk blamelessly before You, walking in the light as He is in the light, we do not walk perfectly (1 John 1:7,8). We give You our hearts anew, confessing once again that we trust only in Christ for our righteousness. We believe that You will, for His sake, keep us from falling and bring us into Your presence with great joy (Rom. 4:5; 10:11; Jude 24,25). Our prayer begins, continues, and ends with our trust in You as the One who initiated our salvation out of Your great love for us while we were sinners, and as the only One who is able, out of that same love, to bring revival (John 3:16; Eph. 2:4; 1 John 4:10). Father, revival will never come if it's left up to us! No person seeks You unless You have first sought him (Rom. 10:20; John 6:44,65)!

Therefore, we ask You to move among Your people within every local church throughout this country and all over the world to bring about the conditions that will result in revival: deep conviction not only of specific sins, but also an awesome revelation of Your presence, leading to a profound sense of the holiness and mightiness of God (John 16:8-10,14; Eph. 1:18-23). Blessed Holy Spirit, be pleased to exalt the most high God, the Lord Jesus Christ, who is the image of the invisible God, the radiance of His glory, and the exact representation of His being (Col. 1:15; Heb. 1:3). Exalt Him who is the creator and sustainer of all things, who is without beginning or end, the firstborn from the dead, who for the sake of the joy set before Him endured the cross, scorning its shame, and now sits at the right hand of the almighty Father (Rev. 21:6; Col. 1:15,16; Heb. 12:2).

Father, it is for Your glory that Your Son humbled Himself and became obedient to death—even death on a cross—so that at His name every knee should bow, in heaven and on earth and under the earth, and every tongue confess that Jesus Christ is LORD (Phil. 2:10-11). We who say we are His, who profess to love Him, who gather in His name week after week, who stake every hope we have of eternal life upon Him, the author and perfecter of our faith, long that He be exalted as Lord in our lives (Heb. 4:14; 12:2; Acts 2:21). May You work in us who call ourselves "believers" to will and to do according to Your good pleasure (Phil. 2:12; Heb. 13:21). May Your grace in our lives not be without effect! May we say with the apostle Paul that we worked harder than all the rest by the grace that You supplied (1 Cor. 15:10). And may we never forget that You redeemed us from an empty way of life with the precious blood of Christ, a Lamb without blemish or defect (1 Peter 2:18,19). Surely, we are not our own; we were bought at a price (1 Cor. 6:20)!

We confess, Father, that we do not love You the way we long to love You (Phil. 3:12-14). We confess that too often the cares, worries, and wealth of this world choke out the life of Christ and keep us from bearing the crop that would please You (Matt. 13:22,23). Make our hearts and minds noble (Luke 8:15). Teach us how to put Christ first (Matt. 6:33). Ignite our hearts with a love for You that does not die out when we leave the worship service but continues as the week unfolds, inspiring us to do good deeds and acts of service through Christ and for His glory (2 Th. 2:16,17). Work in us a perseverance of faith and love (2 Th. 3:5). True revival never just affects our emotions but always leads to an obedience of faith (Deut. 10:12,13; Rom. 16:26). Enable us not to forget Your words, that those who love You obey Your commands (John 14:15). Oh, that we would love Your will as Jesus did (John 6:38)! By Your grace and mercy, may we not miss Your will for revival: the restoration of Your people to their first love, as evidenced by an obedience to all the will of God (1 Peter 1:1,2).

To this end, Father, may You in Your great mercy reveal once again what is needful in every generation of the church: the true gospel. May You take the blindness from our minds, hearts, and wills, to reveal the fact that salvation is from You—a gift that includes repentance from sin and self, and which causes a turning to God by faith in Christ alone as Savior and Lord (Acts 2:38; 17:30; Eph. 6:23; Heb. 5:9; John 3:16). All of this—repentance, turning to God, and faith in Christ as Savior and Lord—is the fruit of the grace of God and the evidence of regeneration (Acts 3:19,20; Eph. 2:8,9).

Salvation is the work solely of God to redeem for Himself a people from every nation, tribe, and language, to become a kingdom and a priesthood to serve Him. For this very purpose, Christ was slain (Rev. 5:9,10; 1 Peter 1:2). By Your Spirit and through Your Word, may You work in us the fruit of the gospel, enabling us to become blameless and pure, children of God in a crooked and depraved generation, in which we shine like stars in the universe as we hold out the Word of Life (Phil. 2:15,16). Father, do establish us by this glorious gospel and by the proclamation of Jesus Christ so that all nations might believe and obey Him (Rom. 16:25).

Finally, Father, we pray that You would illuminate the words of the Bible, that we would reverence them as the very words of God (Psa. 12:6; Matt. 24:35; Psa. 119:89). We confess that we have not studied, memorized, nor believed Your words as sacred, sufficient, and inerrant, the only true guide for all of life and godliness (Deut. 4:2; 12:32; 2 Tim. 3:16; 2 Peter 1:3-4,21). May it be true for us as it was for Him, that we do not live by bread alone but by every word that comes from the mouth of God (Matt. 4:4; Deut. 8:3).

As we close this time of prayer for revival, we pray that this revival will touch not only us who believe, but will serve to bring a multitude into His sheep pen before the end. Our Great Shepherd has other sheep who will listen to His voice, and He will make us one flock with one Shepherd (John 10:16). Remind us, as You did the apostle Paul when he was in Corinth, that You have many people in many places throughout the world (Acts 18:10). May we be compelled by Christ's love, as Paul was, to live no longer for ourselves, but for Him who died for us and was raised again (2 Cor. 5:15). May we, like him, implore others to come to Christ as we fulfill this blessed ministry of reconciliation, that God is reconciling the world to Himself in Christ, not counting men's sins against them (2 Cor. 5:19). Father, You have made us all Christ's ambassadors; may we faithfully, lovingly, and truthfully make Him known, the Lamb of God who was slain for the sins of the world, as You pour Your grace into our lives (2 Cor. 5:20; 1 Tim. 2:5,6; 1 John 2:2; Eph. 4:4-7).

Amen Come, Lord Jesus.

PRAYER FOR REVIVAL OF CHRISTIAN DENOMINATIONS AND GROUPS

Please pray that God will revive these denominations by pouring out the Holy Spirit, bringing about:

1. A knowledge of and adherence to the true gospel: that salvation is by faith in Jesus Christ alone according to the Scriptures.
2. Great love, awe, adoration and praise for Jesus Christ, for the Father and for the Holy Spirit expressed in worship as well as in God-pleasing conduct of life.
3. Passionate concern for the salvation of others and for the relief of poverty and suffering of every kind.
4. The anointing of preachers to preach the gospel and the doctrines of the faith from the Bible with great boldness, clarity, courage and power.
5. Great love among believers evidenced by unity, compassion, forgiveness, forbearance and great generosity.
6. Prayer that is characterized by depth of insight, devotion, love, persistence, frequency and worldwide scope.
7. Holiness of life and obedience to the commandments of the Word of God.
8. Confession of sin and repentance from it as well as the removal of everything that does not please God.
9. Loving shepherds to shepherd the flock with gentleness, kindness, wisdom and love.
10. Unity and love among all believers through Jesus Christ, the Lord.

Adventist Churches: Advent Christian Church; Church of God General Conference; Seventh-Day Adventist Church; Seventh-Day Adventist, Reformed
American Catholic Church
American Rescue Workers
Anglican Churches: Anglican Church in America; Anglican Catholic; Anglican Evangelical Church; Anglican Orthodox Church; Episcopal Church; Reformed Episcopal Church
Apostolic Christian Church of America
Baptist Churches: American Baptist Association (ABA); American

Baptist Churches in the USA; Baptist Bible Fellowship International; Baptist General Conference; Baptist Missionary Association of America; Conservative Baptist Association of America; Free Will Baptists; General Association of General Baptists; General Association of Regular Baptist Churches (GARBC); National Baptist Convention; National Missionary Baptist Convention of America; North American Baptist Conference; Primitive Baptists; Progressive National Baptist Convention; Separate Baptists in Christ; Southern Baptist Convention; Seventh-Day Baptist General Conference; Sovereign Grace Believers

Berean Fundamental Church

Bible Churches

Brethren (German Baptists): Brethren Church (Ashland, Ohio); Church of the Brethren; Grace Brethren Churches; Old German Baptist Brethren

Brethren, River: Brethren in Christ; United Zion Church

Byzantine Catholic

Charismatic Churches

Christian Brethren (Plymouth Brethren)

Christian Church (Disciples of Christ)

Christian Churches of North America

Christian Congregation, Inc.

Christian and Missionary Alliance

Christian Union, Churches of Christ

Church of Christ in Christian Union

Church of Christ (Holiness)

Church of the United Brethren in Christ

Churches of Christ

Churches of God: Church of God, General Conference; Church of God (Anderson, Indiana); Church of God, Seventh Day; Church of God by Faith, Inc.; Church of God, Mountain Assembly

Church of the Nazarene

Community Churches

Congregational Christian Churches

Conservative Congregational Christian Conference

Covenant Churches

Eastern Orthodox Churches: Albanian Orthodox; American Carpatho-
Russian Orthodox Greek Catholic; Antiochian Orthodox Chris-
tian; Apostolic Catholic Assyrian Church of the East; Armenian
Apostolic Church of America; Diocese of America; Armenian
Church; Coptic Orthodox Church; Greek Orthodox; Malankara
Mar Thoma Synan Church, Diocese of North America and
Europe; Orthodox Church in America; Romanian Orthodox;
Russian Orthodox Church outside of Russia; Serbian Orthodox
Church; Syrian Orthodox Church of Antioch; Ukranian Orthodox
Church
Evangelical Church
Evangelical Congregational Church
Evangelical Covenant Church
Evangelical Free Church
Friends: Evangelical Friends International; Friends General Conference;
Friends United Meeting; Religious Society of Friends (Conserva-
tive)
Full Gospel Fellowship
Grace Gospel Fellowship
Independent Churches
Independent Bible Churches
Independent Fundamental Churches of America (IFCA)
Interdenominational
Jewish Christian
Liberal Catholic Church
Lutheran Churches: American Association of Lutheran Churches;
Apostolic Lutheran Church of America (ALCA); Church of the
Lutheran Brethren of America; Church of the Lutheran Confes-
sion; Evangelical Lutheran Church in America (ELCA); Evan-
gelical Lutheran Synod; Free Lutheran Congregations; Latvian
Evangelical Lutheran Church in America; Lutheran Church,
Missouri Synod; Wisconsin Evangelical Lutheran Synod
Mennonite Churches: Beachy Amish Mennonite; Church of God in
Christ (Mennonite); Evangelical Mennonite Church; Hutterian
Brethren; Mennonite Brethren Churches, General Conference;
Mennonite Church; Mennonite Church, General Conference; Old

Order Amish Churches

Methodist Churches: African Methodist Episcopal; African Methodist Episcopal Zion Church; Bible Holiness Church; Christian Methodist Episcopal Church; Evangelical Methodist Church; Free Methodist Church of North America; Primitive Methodist Church in the USA; Southern Methodist Church; United Methodist Church; The Wesleyan Church

Metropolitan Community Churches

Missionary Church

Moravian Churches: Moravian Church in America, North Province

National Organization of the New Apostolic Church of North America

Non-denominational Churches

Old Catholic Churches

Pentecostal Churches: Apostolic Faith Mission Church of God; Apostolic Overcoming Holy Catholic Church of God, Inc.; Assemblies of God; Bible Church of Christ; Bible Fellowship Church; Church of God (Cleveland, Tennessee); Church of God in Christ; Church of God of Prophecy; Elim Fellowship, Intl.; Church of the Foursquare Gospel; International Pentecostal Church of Christ; International Pentecostal Holiness Church; Open Bible Standard Churches; Pentecostal Assemblies of the World, Inc.; Pentecostal Church of God; Pentecostal Free Will Baptist Church; United Pentecostal Church International

Pillar of Fire Churches

Polish National Catholic Church

Presbyterian Churches: Assoc. Reformed Presbyterian Church (General Synod); Cumberland Presbyterian Church; Cumberland Presbyterian Church in America; Evangelical Presbyterian Church; General Assembly of the Korean Presbyterian Church in America; Orthodox Presbyterian Church; Presbyterian Church in America; Presbyterian Church (USA); Reformed Presbyterian Church of North America

Reformed Churches: Christian Reformed Church in North America; Hungarian Reformed Church in North America; Netherland Reformed Congregations; Protestant Reformed Churches in America; Reformed Church in America; United Church of Christ

Reformed Episcopal Church
Roman Catholic Church
Salvation Army
Ukranian Catholic
Vineyard Christian Fellowship
Wesleyan Holiness Association of Churches
World Wide Church of God

PRAYER FOR PERSECUTED BELIEVERS

Believers are being persecuted in the following fifty-seven nations of the world, with little or no protection from their governments. Pray that God will strengthen and protect them, enable them to glorify Christ, and give them words to make known the gospel with boldness, clarity, courage and fearlessness. Pray that God will meet all their needs according to His glorious riches in Christ Jesus. Ask that He protect them from the Evil One. Pray that He will minister to those who are in prison and that they may be released and set free. Also, pray that God will change the governments of these nations so that Christians will be able to live in peace and proclaim the gospel freely by their lives and testimonies.

Africa – Algeria, Chad, Comoros Islands, Djibouti, Egypt, Equatorial Guinea, Ethiopia, Libya, Mauritania, Morocco, Nigeria, Somalia, Sudan and Tunisia

Asia – Afghanistan, Bangladesh, Bhutan, Brunei, Cambodia, China, India, Indonesia, Laos, Malaysia, Maldives, Myanmar, Nepal, North Korea, Pakistan, Philippines, Sri Lanka, Tibet and Vietnam

Caribbean – Cuba

Eurasia – Azerbaijan, Chechnya, Russia, Tajikistan, Turkmenistan, and Uzbekistan

Latin America – Colombia, Mexico (Chiapas) and Peru

Middle East – Bahrain, Cyprus, Iran, Iraq, Israel, Jordan, Kuwait, Oman, Qatar, Saudi Arabia, Syria, Turkey, United Arab Emirates and Yemen

NAMES OF BELIEVERS

Please use this space to list the names of believers, including yourself, your family, the members of your extended family who are believers, your believing friends, your local church, your pastor, other leaders in your church, the members of your congregation, other ministries and churches, missionaries, mission boards, Christian schools including administration, faculty, and students, and so forth.

NAMES OF BELIEVERS

NAMES OF BELIEVERS

NAMES OF BELIEVERS

PERSONAL PRAYER REQUESTS

PERSONAL PRAYER REQUESTS

ANSWERS TO PRAYER

ANSWERS TO PRAYER

PRAYING FOR THE LOST

I urge, then, first of all, that requests, prayers, intercession, and thanksgiving be made for everyone – for kings and all those in authority, that we may live peaceful and quiet lives in all godliness and holiness. This is good, and pleases God our Savior, who wants all men to be saved and to come to a knowledge of the truth.
1 Timothy 2:1-4

PRAYING FOR THE LOST

There are seven chapters in this section:
1. *An Overview of God's Will for the Lost* – A summary of God's will regarding salvation to be used in prayer.
2. *Salvation Verses and Prayers for the Lost* – A selection of verses followed by prayers for the lost.
3. *My List of the Lost* – The names of people I am asking God to save.
4. *List of the Lost (General)* – Prayers asking God to save people from false religions, cults, new religious movements, and other organizations.
5. *Prayer for Our Nation* – Intercessory prayer for the sins of our nation, asking God for good government and for the salvation of many within our nation.
6. *Prayer for the Nations of the World* – Intercession for all the nations of the world.
7. *Maps and Lists of the Nations of the world.*

HOW TO USE THIS SECTION

Use this section of the book in exactly the same way you have used the previous sections, by reading a few verses and prayers, asking God to save the lost throughout the world according to His Word.

Following the chapter *Salvation Verses and Prayers for the Lost* is a chapter entitled *My List of the Lost: People I Am Asking God to Save.* This chapter provides space where you can list the people you care about, whom you desire God to save by enabling them to have personal faith in and obedience to Jesus Christ. Dare to name anyone! On my list, I've included the names of practically everyone I have ever known, including all my relatives and many of the famous people I've come to care about over the years—people in the motion picture and television industries, politicians, government officials, heads of state, and so on. I also include the people I come into contact with during my day—those who work in the stores where I shop, my dentist, doctor, neighbors, boss, coworkers, hairdresser, and so forth.

Since I cannot know whom God has chosen—and since I know that none of us are worthy to be saved and that Christ has done all the work necessary—it is my joy to pray for as many people as possible, trusting in God's promises concerning His will (i.e., that according to 1 Timothy 2:4, He wants all men to be saved) and in the sufficiency of Christ's work. My trust is not in the people and their worthiness, but in Christ and His worthiness.

After this comes a chapter titled *List of the Lost (General)*, which is a place for you to list those in false religions, cults, new religious movements, and other organizations. Ask God to bring to salvation many people from each, enabling them to believe in Christ alone for salvation according to the Scriptures.

Praying for our nation and for the world follows the same idea. God wants us to pray for those in authority and links good government with salvation:

> I urge, then, first of all, that requests, prayers, intercession and thanksgiving be made for everyone—for kings and all those in authority, that we may live peaceful and quiet lives in all godliness and holiness. This is good, and pleases God our Savior, who wants all men to be saved and to come to a knowledge of the truth. (1 Tim. 2:1-4)

The Lord also wants us to pray for the nations: "'Ask of Me, and I will make the nations your inheritance, the ends of the earth your possession'" (Ps. 2:8). We have only to believe Him—that He knows every single person on the face of the earth! Our trust is not at all in ourselves but in Him—His love, power, knowledge and mercy to all men because of Jesus Christ, the Lord.

Therefore, whether you are praying for individuals or for nations, simply find verses from this chapter and tell God that your prayer is for the following people and nations as you name them to Him; ask Him to accomplish His will for His glory: the salvation of the lost from every tribe, language, nation and people (Rev. 5:9-10). *Believe in His promises, and you will see Him do great things!*

> Now to Him who is able to do immeasurably more than all we ask or imagine, according to His power that is at work within us, to Him be glory in the church and in Christ Jesus throughout all generations, for ever and ever! Amen (Eph. 3:20,21)

ABOUT PRAYING FOR THE LOST

The Lord Jesus Christ gave one final command before He ascended into heaven after His resurrection from death:

> "All authority in heaven and on earth has been given to Me. Therefore go and make disciples of all nations, baptizing them in the name of the Father and of the Son and of the Holy Spirit, and teaching them to obey everything I have commanded you. And surely I am with you always, to the very end of the age." (Matt. 28:18-20)

Jesus' will was that we go and make disciples, that is, that we bring about an obedience of faith among those with whom we share the gospel. This is why the apostle Paul wrote, "Through Him and for His name's sake, we received grace and apostleship to call people from among all the Gentiles to the obedience that comes from faith" (Rom. 1:5). Only God can bring someone to Himself (John 6:43,65). Only God knows whom He has predestined, called, justified and glorified in Christ Jesus (Rom. 8:30). Our prayers are our cooperation with Him to work out His purposes on earth as He wills. Our example is the Lord's Prayer: "Your kingdom come, Your will be done on earth as it is in heaven" (Matt. 6:10). Just as it is through us that He spreads the gospel, it is also through our prayers that He accomplishes the calling unto Himself of His chosen ones. All of this is in reliance upon His Spirit and the Word of God. Our job is to believe and ask according to His will.

When we enter into God's will for the world by praying in this way for the lost, we fulfill our role as priests (1 Peter 2:5,9). What does a priest do for his people according to the Scriptures? He represents them to God with sacrifices for sins (Heb. 5:1). Christ Jesus has offered one sacrifice for all time—His blood and body for our sins (Heb. 9:28)—and not only for ours but also for the sins of the whole world (1 John 2:2). He lives forever to intercede for us before God (Heb. 7:25). In Him, God has made us to be priests as well, offering spiritual sacrifices to Him of our bodies, our gifts, our praises and our good works (Rev. 5:10). But God has also required us to intercede as Christ does for men before Him (1 Tim. 2:1). This work of intercession is made possible because God has raised us up with Christ and seated us in the heavenly realms with Him (Eph. 2:6). In our union with Him, we are to represent men on earth before the Father, pleading for them just as Christ does by pointing to His blood and body on their behalf. This is intercessory prayer.

May our precious Lord direct your heart into this most blessed ministry of intercession! And may you live such a consecrated life unto Him that whatever you ask for in prayer, He will give you for the Father's glory—and for your joy! (See John 15:7,8; 16:24.)

AN OVERVIEW OF GOD'S WILL FOR THE LOST

May You, the LORD God, save unbelievers everywhere both near and far because:

1. You are merciful. (Titus 3:5)

2. You are loving and faithful. (Psa. 108:4)

3. You blot out transgressions for Your own sake. (Isa. 43:25)

4. You are compassionate, gracious and slow to anger. You abound in love and faithfulness and maintain love to thousands. You forgive wickedness, rebellion and sin. (Ex. 34:6,7,9)

5. You do not treat anyone as his sins deserve or repay him according to his iniquities. (Psa. 103:10)

6. You love everyone and are a God of grace. (Eph. 2:4,5)

7. Christ died for the ungodly, for sinners. (Rom. 5:6-8)

8. Christ died for sins, once for all. (1 Peter 3:18)

9. You so love this world that You gave Your Son. (John 3:16)

10. You justify everyone who does not work but trusts in You. (Rom. 4:4,5)

11. It is Your will to set prisoners free, to give sight to the blind, to release the oppressed, and to proclaim your favor; this is why Jesus came. (Luke 4:18,19)

12. You want all men to be saved, and You gave Your Son as a ransom for all men. (1 Tim. 2:3-6)

13. He is the atoning sacrifice for the sins of the whole world, not just for the sins of those who already believe. (1 John 2:2)

14. You have asked us to ask of You, that You make the nations of the world and the ends of the earth His possession. (Psa. 2:8)

15. Christ's death on the cross and His shed blood are worthy to purchase men for God from every tribe, language, people and nation. (Rev. 5:9)

16. His blood fulfills the requirement of the law for the forgiveness of sin. (Heb. 9:22)

17. You invite everyone to call on the name of the Lord and be saved. (Acts 2:21)

18. Jesus said that He had other sheep not yet of the sheep pen and that He must bring them also. He promised that they, too, would listen to His voice. (John 10:14-16)

19. It is Your will. Jesus's last commandment was that we who are His disciples should go and make disciples of all nations, teaching them to obey everything He had commanded. (Matt. 28:18-20)

20. The Holy Spirit was given. (on the day of Pentecost) to empower us to be Christ's witnesses from Jerusalem, in all Judea and Samaria, and to the ends of the earth. (Acts 1:8)

Because You want sinners to be saved, we, Your priests, ask You, heavenly Father, to do the following:

1. Take the blindness from unbelievers' minds because the devil has blinded them. (2 Cor. 4:4)

2. Convict them of sin, righteousness and judgement through the ministry of the Holy Spirit. (John 16:8)

3. Enable sinners to be drawn to Christ, because no one comes to the Savior unless the Father draws him. (John 6:43,65)

4. Send born-again Christians out to tell the gospel, because sinners can't believe in Christ if they have not heard of Him and what He has done. (Rom. 10:14,17)

5. Send out workers because the harvest is plentiful but the workers are few. (Matt. 9:37,38)

6. Open a door for the message of the gospel. Enable us to proclaim it clearly as we should. Enable us to be wise around outsiders and to make the most of every opportunity. Remind us to be full of Your grace, to be salt, and to be able to answer everyone. (Col. 4:3-6)

7. Show us where You are at work around us so that we may join You, for we can do nothing on our own. (John 5:19,20)

8. Enable us to have courage to exalt Christ in our bodies, whether by death or life. (Phil. 1:20)

9. Fulfill Your promise that when we ask anything according to Your will—and the salvation of the lost is Your will—that You hear us and will give us what we ask of You. (1 John 5:14,15)

10. Bring glory to the Father, Lord Jesus, by doing what we ask of You: save the lost. (John 14:13,14)

11. Save the lost because two or more of us agree that it is Your will. (Matt. 18:19)

12. Save our loved ones because we remain in You and Your words remain in us—and because it is for Your glory that we bear much fruit. (John 15:7,8)

13. Save unbelievers because our hearts do not condemn us; we are obeying Your commandments and doing what pleases You. (1 John 3:21,22)

14. Save the lost so that our joy will be complete. (John 16:24)

15. Save those who look as if they are impossible to save, because we believe that all things are possible with God. (Matt. 19:23-26)

16. Save as many of the lost as possible because Christ is worthy. (Rev. 5:12)

SALVATION VERSES AND
PRAYERS FOR THE LOST

He saved us, not because of righteous things we had done, but because of His mercy...(Titus 3:5)

> Dear heavenly Father,
> Just as You saved us because of Your mercy, save our loved ones. Forgive us, those who already believe, for self-righteousness. For we were once just like the lost, and it was Your mercy, not our righteousness, that saved us.
>
> Amen

For great is Your love, higher than the heavens; Your faithfulness reaches to the skies. (Psa. 108:4)

> Dear heavenly Father,
> We believe and trust in Your character—Your love that is higher than the heavens and Your faithfulness that reaches to the skies—to save those who do not believe. Only because of Your love and faithfulness can anyone find salvation!
>
> Amen

"I, even I, am He who blots out your transgressions, for My own sake, and remembers your sins no more." (Isa. 43:25)

> Dear heavenly Father,
> Please blot out the transgressions of my family members, friends, and neighbors who do not yet believe in You! Please remember their sins no more, for the sake of Christ Jesus, who died for them!
>
> In Christ's name, Amen

And He passed in front of Moses, proclaiming, "The LORD, the LORD, the compassionate and gracious God, slow to anger, abounding in love and faithfulness, maintaining love to thousands, and forgiving wickedness, rebellion and sin. O Lord, if I have found favor in your eyes," He said, "then let the Lord go with us. Although this is a stiff-necked people, forgive our wickedness and our sin, and take us as your inheritance." (Ex. 34:6,7,9)

Dear heavenly Father,

Forgive thousands today because You are gracious; abounding in love and faithfulness; maintaining love to thousands; forgiving wickedness, rebellion, and sin. And may it be so because we who are priests with Christ have found favor in Your eyes. Take the lost as Your inheritance because of Your character, because of Your worthiness, and because of our walk with You. May the priesthood of believers' prayers avail much today, even as Moses' priestly prayer availed much for his people.

In Christ we pray, Amen

He does not treat us as our sins deserve or repay us according to our iniquities. (Psa. 103:10)

Dear heavenly Father,

For all those who are without Christ and are lost in sin and death, please do not treat them as their sins deserve or repay them according to their iniquities. Instead, treat them according to Your character of love!

Amen

But because of His great love for us, God, who is rich in mercy, made us alive with Christ even when we were dead in transgressions—it is by grace you have been saved. (Eph. 2:4,5)

Dear heavenly Father,

Oh, precious Father, thank You for Your great love for us and for Your incredible mercy by which You made us alive with Christ when we were dead in sin. How we pray that Your great love may reach many more around us! We pray for them because of Christ and His worthiness, for He truly is the mercy of God.

Amen

You see, at just the right time, when we were still powerless, Christ died for the ungodly. Very rarely will anyone die for a righteous man, though for a good man someone might possibly dare to die. But God demonstrates His own love for us in this: While we were still sinners, Christ died for us. (Rom. 5:6-8)

> Dear heavenly Father,
>
> We acknowledge that just as we were powerless to save ourselves, so are all those around us who are not yet saved. We pray that they might know that Christ died for them, just as He died for us. We plead for them through Christ and His shed blood.
>
> In Jesus' name, Amen

For Christ died for sins once for all, the righteous for the unrighteous, to bring you to God...(1 Peter 3:18)

> Dear heavenly Father,
>
> Since Christ died for sins once for all, we ask that You apply His work to the following people, so that they, like us, will be brought to You: (List the names of people you desire to be saved).
>
> For the sake of Christ Jesus, who is worthy, Amen

For God so loved the world that He gave His one and only Son, that whoever believes in Him shall not perish but have eternal life. (John 3:16)

> Dearest loving Father,
>
> According to this verse, it is our faith in Your Son that gives us eternal life. We pray that You will enable those who do not yet believe in Him to have faith in Him, so that they may not perish but have eternal life. May Your love in sending Jesus be received by as many people as possible.
>
> For the sake of Jesus, Amen

Now when a man works, his wages are not credited to him as a gift, but as an obligation. However, to the man who does not work but trusts in God who justifies the wicked, his faith is credited as righteousness. (Rom. 4:4,5)

> Dear Father,

We pray that You will give understanding to unbelievers everywhere to see that good works are not the way to be made right with God—but rather, that we are made right only when we trust in God—a God so wonderful that He justifies the wicked! How we thank You!

Amen

"The Spirit of the Lord is on Me, because he has anointed Me to preach good news to the poor. He has sent Me to proclaim freedom for the prisoners and recovery of sight for the blind, to release the oppressed, to proclaim the year of the Lord's favor." (Luke 4:18,19)

Dear Jesus,

You spoke these words from Isaiah 61 as You began Your public ministry and ushered in the messianic age, the period when salvation would be proclaimed. We pray that we who are Your body—Your mouth, hands, and feet—will also proclaim the good news of the Lord's favor. And we affirm in this prayer that it was Your will then, as it is now, that the captives be set free!

With thanksgiving, Amen

This is good, and pleases God our Savior, who wants all men to be saved and to come to a knowledge of the truth. For there is one God and one mediator between God and men, the man Christ Jesus, who gave Himself as a ransom for all men—the testimony given in its proper time. (1 Tim. 2:3-6)

Dear heavenly Father,

What a wonderful promise! You want all men to know the truth: Christ gave Himself as a ransom for all men! Therefore, we apply Your will and Christ's work to the following people and ask that You save them: (names of people). How we thank You for hearing our prayer.

In Christ's name, Amen

He is the atoning sacrifice for our sins, and not only for ours but also for the sins of the whole world. (1 John 2:2)

Dear heavenly Father,

Since You have given Christ as an atoning sacrifice for the sins of the whole world, we apply His sacrifice to every nation on earth and pray that many within each nation come to believe in Him, just as we do. We know one thing: Jesus has already done it all! The payment He made is sufficient; may it now prove to be effective!

In His name, Amen

Ask of Me, and I will make the nations your inheritance, the ends of the earth your possession. (Psa. 2:8)

Dear heavenly Father,

We do ask that You make the nations of the world His inheritance and the ends of the earth His possession—because He is worthy! He is worthy that every single person in every nation on the face of this earth bow his knee and worship Him forever.

In Your name, O Lord, Amen

..."You are worthy to take the scroll and to open its seals, because You were slain, and with Your blood You purchased men for God from every tribe and language and people and nation." (Rev. 5:9)

Dearest heavenly Father,

Because of Christ's worthiness and because of the sufficiency of His blood, we ask You to purchase men for Yourself from every tribe, language, people and nation. May You honor the sacrifice of Your Son.

In the Lamb's name and for His sake, Amen

In fact, the law requires that nearly everything be cleansed with blood and without the shedding of blood there is no forgiveness. (Heb. 9:22)

Dear holy and righteous Father,

Oh, but we have the perfect blood of Jesus to plead before Your throne on behalf of the lost! We do not come before You except by our faith in Your Son's blood. How thankful we are for the perfection of His blood! We cover the whole world in the blood of Your Son. May His blood cover the sins of multitudes before the end.

Amen

And everyone who calls on the name of the Lord will be saved. (Acts 2:21)

> Dear merciful Father,
>
> How gracious You are that all sinners have to do is call on the name of Your Son! That is because He has paid the price for everyone. Enable sinners to call! Send believers out to tell of His name, for how can they call on One of whom they have never heard?
>
> In the name of Jesus, Amen

"I am the good shepherd; I know My sheep and My sheep know Me—just as the Father knows Me and I know the Father—and I lay down My life for the sheep. I have other sheep that are not of this sheep pen. I must bring them also. They too will listen to My voice, and there shall be one flock and one shepherd." (John 10:14-16)

> Dear Great Shepherd,
>
> Call Your other sheep, those who have not yet received You. You have promised that they will hear You. Bring them into the flock, and make us one flock with one Shepherd.
>
> For Your sake we pray, Amen

Then Jesus came to them and said, "All authority in heaven and on earth has been given to Me. Therefore go and make disciples of all nations, baptizing them in the name of the Father and of the Son and of the Holy Spirit, and teaching them to obey everything I have commanded you. And surely I am with you always, to the very end of the age." (Matt. 28:18-20)

> Dear Lord,
>
> Your last command to Your disciples was that, because of the authority that had been given to You by virtue of Your victory at the cross, they were to go to all nations, making disciples, baptizing them in the name of the Father, the Son, and the Holy Spirit, and teaching them to obey everything You commanded. And You promised to be with them always, to the very end of the age. This command and this promise are for us as well, for we too are Your disciples. Oh, Lord Jesus, fill all Your disciples with a passion to obey this command! Fill us with the Holy Spirit so that we experi-

ence Your presence and reach the lost with Your love, truth, and words! And remind us that, like an ambassador who goes in the authority of his country, we go in Your authority, not ours!

For Your sake, Amen

"But you will receive power when the Holy Spirit comes on you; and you will be My witnesses in Jerusalem, and in all Judea and Samaria, and to the ends of the earth." (Acts 1:8)

Dearest Lord Jesus,

Thank You so much for not leaving us alone when You ascended into heaven to sit at the right hand of God, but for sending the Holy Spirit to give us the power to fulfill Your last command! Enable us to believe and to live righteous lives, so that You will fill us with Your Spirit, enabling us to be powerful witnesses of the gospel all over the world—in our neighborhoods, cities, states, nation and all over the world.

For Your sake and for Your glory, Amen

The god of this age has blinded the minds of unbelievers, so they cannot see the light of the gospel of the glory of Christ, who is the image of God. (2 Cor. 4:4)

Dear heavenly Father,

Please have mercy on unbelievers just as You did on us before we believed. We too were at one time blinded by the devil. But in Your mercy, You took the blindness from our minds so that we could believe in Christ and be saved. Do the same for unbelievers everywhere!

For the glory of Your Son, Amen

When He comes, He will convict the world of guilt in regard to sin and righteousness and judgment...(John 16:8)

Dear Holy Spirit,

We pray for Your work to be powerful in convicting unbelievers all over the world that they are sinners who need the righteousness that can only come by believing in Christ and His death on the cross. Only someone who knows he is a sinner feels his need for a Savior!

For Christ's sake, Amen

"No one can come to Me unless the Father who sent Me draws him, and I will raise him up at the last day." He went on to say, "This is why I told you that no one can come to Me unless the Father has enabled him." (John 6:44,65)

Dear heavenly Father,

According to these verses, no one can come to Christ unless You enable him. Therefore, we pray that You will draw unbelievers to Christ, enabling them to believe in Him, Your precious Son, and raising them up on the last day.

For the glory of Your Son, Amen

How, then, can they call on the one they have not believed in? And how can they believe in the one of whom they have not heard? And how can they hear without someone preaching to them? And how can they preach unless they are sent? As it is written, "How beautiful are the feet of those who bring good news!" Consequently, faith comes from hearing the message, and the message is heard through the word of Christ. (Rom. 10:14,15,17)

Dear heavenly Father,

According to these verses, no one can believe in Christ in order to be saved unless they hear the gospel. Therefore, we pray that You will send us out to give the Gospel to everyone. May our faith in these verses compel us to make known the Gospel!

In Christ's Name, Amen

"The harvest is plentiful but the workers are few. Ask the Lord of the harvest, therefore, to send out the workers into his harvest field." (Matt. 9:37,38)

Dear Father,

Here is Your promise to us that the harvest is plentiful. But since the workers are few, please send us out, and others all over the world, to bring in the harvest of salvation that You have prepared.

For His sake, Amen

And pray for us, too, that God may open a door for our message, so that we may proclaim the mystery of Christ…Pray that I may proclaim it clearly as I should. Be wise in the way you act toward outsiders; make the most of every opportunity. Let your conversation be always full of grace, seasoned with salt, so that you may know how to answer everyone (Col. 4:3-6)

Dear heavenly Father,

We do pray that You will open a door for us to tell the Gospel to someone. We also pray for everyone else around the world who is doing the work of an evangelist, whether lay person, pastor or missionary. Open up the door for the message of the Gospel everywhere and in every nation. We pray that You will enable everyone who shares the message of Christ to proclaim it clearly as he should. Remind us, also, to be wise around unbelievers and to make the most of every opportunity. Make our conversation full of grace and seasoned with salt.

According to the will of God, Amen

…"I tell you the truth, the Son can do nothing by Himself; He can do only what He sees His Father doing, because whatever the Father does the Son also does. For the Father loves the Son and shows Him all He does." (John 5:19,20)

Dearest heavenly Father,

If the Son of God could do nothing by Himself but only what He saw You doing, then how much more must we look to see what You are doing! And because You love us as You love the Son, You will show us all You are doing just as You showed Him. Then we will join You.

Amen

I eagerly expect and hope that I will in no way be ashamed, but will have sufficient courage so that now as always Christ will be exalted in my body, whether by life or by death. For to me, to live is Christ and to die is gain. (Phil. 1:20,21)

> Dear heavenly Father,
>
> Give all of us who believe in You this same attitude as the Apostle Paul's! With this attitude the Gospel will surely be invincible!
>
> In the Name that is above all names, Amen

This is the confidence we have in approaching God: that if we ask anything according to His will, He hears us. And if we know that He hears us—whatever we ask—we know that we have what we asked of Him. (1 John 5:14,15)

> Dear heavenly Father,
>
> What an incredible promise! According to these verses, You will answer our prayers for the lost because we know from the word of God that it is Your will that none might perish. So we lift up to You the names of these people that we love. We believe that You hear us and therefore that You will save them.
>
> In the Son of God who died for all, Amen

And I will do whatever you ask in My name, so that the Son may bring glory to the Father. You may ask Me for anything in My name, and I will do it. (John 14:13,14)

> Dear Savior, Lord Jesus,
>
> Bring glory to the Father by saving our loved ones and others from every nation of the world—glorify the Father by answering our prayer!
>
> For His sake, Amen

"Again, I tell you that if two of you on earth agree about anything you ask for, it will be done for you by My Father in heaven." (Matt. 18:19)

> Dear heavenly Father,
>
> Honor the promise of Your Son. Answer our prayers for the lost because two or more of us agree.
>
> In Christ's promise, Amen

"If you remain in Me and My words remain in you, ask whatever you wish, and it will be given you. This is to My Father's glory, that you bear much fruit, showing yourselves to be My disciples." (John 15:7,8)

> Dear heavenly Father,
>
> It is because we remain in Your Son and His words remain in us that we ask You for the salvation of the lost. We would not desire salvation for others unless His will and desire had become ours! We are asking according to His will and for Your glory because we are His disciples. Therefore, glorify Yourself by enabling us to bear much fruit, the salvation of the lost.
>
> For Your glory, Amen

Dear friends, if our hearts do not condemn us, we have confidence before God and receive from Him anything we ask, because we obey His commands and do what pleases Him. (1 John 3:21,22)

> Dear heavenly Father,
>
> Answer our prayers for the lost because our hearts do not condemn us. We are living in obedience to Your commands and doing everything we can to please You. And for those Christians whose hearts condemn them, show them what they need to do to be right with You. Convict them of how much is at stake! It is really so easy to be right with You. It means giving You the Lordship of our lives, finding out Your commands and doing them by Your strength, believing that we are new creations willing and able to please You because we have been born-again, living by the Spirit and not trying to obey You as if we were still under "law," listening to our conscience and never doing anything that hurts it, and most of all, loving You with all our heart, mind, soul and strength. Love covers a multitude of sins! In Christ who covers our hearts with His blood and lives forever to intercede for us,
>
> Amen

"Until now you have not asked for anything in My name. Ask and you will receive, and your joy will be complete." (John 16:24)

Dear heavenly Father,

We ask in Your Son's matchless name: answer our prayers for the salvation of the lost. Make our joy complete by giving Christ the largest inheritance possible!

In the Name above all names, Amen

Then Jesus said to His disciples, "I tell you the truth, it is hard for a rich man to enter the kingdom of heaven. Again I tell you, it is easier for a camel to go through the eye of a needle than for a rich man to enter the kingdom of God." When the disciples heard this, they were greatly astonished and asked, "Who then can be saved?" Jesus looked at them and said, "With man this is impossible, but with God all things are possible." (Matt. 19:23-26)

Dearest heavenly Father,

We believe that nothing is impossible for God! Answer our prayers for the lost according to our faith in You. And show us, too, that it is not just the rich who seem impossible but so many others as well. Nevertheless, all things are possible with God! Increase the faith of the weak who tend to look at the unbeliever instead of at You. Enable us to believe in You. Convince us through the Word how great You are!

In the name of the Lord, for whom nothing is impossible, Amen

"Worthy is the Lamb, who was slain, to receive power and wealth and wisdom and strength and honor and glory and praise!" (Rev. 5:12)

Dear heavenly Father,

Save as many as possible from this earth because Christ Jesus, Your Son, is worthy!

In the name of the Messiah, the Lamb of God, Amen

MY LIST OF THE LOST:
PEOPLE I AM ASKING GOD TO SAVE

Please use this space to list everyone you can think of, including everyone in your family and extended family, neighbors, friends, and people at work; those who serve you at restaurants, in shops, and at the grocery store; people you sit next to at sporting events; those who serve with you on committees; classmates; those to whom you and your church are ministering; people you have met only once or twice; and those who live far away.

Look around with the eyes of Jesus, and see people as He sees them—lost and without hope if they do not know Him. Pray in the way He is praying in heaven, asking His Father to save them for His sake.

MY LIST OF THE LOST

MY LIST OF THE LOST

MY LIST OF THE LOST

LIST OF THE LOST (GENERAL)

Please use this chapter to ask God to save people in non-Christian religions, cults and other organizations.

"Now this is eternal life: that they may know You, the only true God, and Jesus Christ, whom You have sent." (John 17:3)

"The god of this age has blinded the minds of unbelievers, so that they cannot see the light of the gospel of the glory of Christ, who is the image of God." (2 Cor. 4:4)

1. Prayer for Those in Non-Christian Religions

Islam, Buddhism, Hinduism, Taoism, Judaism, Secularism, New Age Movement, Animism, Confucianism, Marxism and Shinto.

2. Prayer for Those in Cults and New Religious Movements

Mormonism, Baha'i, Edgar Cayce and the Association for Research and Enlightenment, Christian Science, Church Universal and Triumphant, The Divine Life Society/Integral Yoga Institute, Divine Light Mission/Elan Vital, Eckankar, The Family/Children of God, Human Potential Seminars (Est/The Forum, Lifespring, Actualizations, Momentus), Jehovah's Witnesses, The Local Church, The Masonic Lodge, Ram Dass, Religious Science (Science of the Mind), Rosicrucian Fellowship, Scientology, Silva Mind Control, Sufism, Theosophy and the Theosophical Society, Tibetan Buddhism, Transcendental Meditation, UFO's and UFO Cults, Unification Church, Unitarian Universalism, Unity School of Christianity, The Way International, Zen, etc.

3. Prayer for Those in Secular Organizations

Pray for secular organizations such as the following: National Organization of Women (NOW), American Civil Liberties Union (ACLU), American Psychiatric Assoc. (APA), National Abortion Rights Action League (NARAL), National Man Boy Love Association (NAMBLA), Planned Parenthood, People for the American Way, Parents/Friends of Lesbians and Gays (PFLAG), Greenpeace and other groups that think that salvation comes through environmentalism, American Medical Association (AMA), etc. Pray for professional organizations associated with your work, in the media, in sports, etc.

Prayer for Our Nation

Dear heavenly Father,

We come to You today to plead for our nation, which surely deserves only Your wrath and judgment. We name the sins of godlessness; secularization at all levels of society; materialism, sexual immorality; perversion of sex, truth, power and authority; homosexuality; alcohol and drug abuse; lawlessness; divorce; gambling; fiscal irresponsibility and debt; moral depravity among the television and motion picture industries; crime; religious liberalism and token Christianity; rebellion of every kind; racism; involvement in the occult and outright satanic worship; lack of compassion for the poor; abortion; the abandonment of our children to the evils of worldly peer pressure; and wickedness of every kind.

We ask You to forgive our nation because of Christ's blood, for "He is the atoning sacrifice for our sins, and not only for ours but also for the sins of the whole world" (1 John 2:2). The people of our nation are blinded by the devil's schemes (2 Cor. 4:4) and cannot come to You themselves. But we, as priests of God (Rev. 5:10), intercede for them.

Father, we are so grateful that You are the God of all grace, love, and compassion (Psa. 108:4). We ask You to convict this nation of sin and bring her to repentance. If You must judge, we ask that You begin with the church (Heb. 10:30). Discipline those of us who have Your Word and Your Spirit! Revive us so that our nation may turn from its wickedness and find You.

Truly, we pray for the people of this land as Jesus prayed: "Father, forgive them, for they do not know what they are doing" (Luke 23:34). We claim Your own character and goodness on behalf of our nation according to Your Word: "I, even I, am He who blots out your transgressions, for My own sake, and remembers your sins no more." (Isa. 43:25). The greatest glory for Your Son would be for You to bring a great and mighty revival that would serve to restore this nation to "one nation under God, indivisible, with liberty and justice for all." Therefore, glorify Your Son!

Father, we also pray for the following people and situations in our land. We know that You connect good government with the salvation of the lost (1 Tim. 2:1-4), and so we pray for good government:

1. Please protect, guide, and keep the president of the United States and give him wisdom. Protect and keep him and his family from the evil one. Make him Your messenger of good, not evil. (Rom. 13:1,4)

2. Give wisdom to all Cabinet heads and Cabinet members.

3. Guide and give wisdom to the U.S. Congress—members of both the Senate and the House—and all its leaders.

4. In upcoming elections at every level, please put into authority God-fearing men and women. Remove from authority all those who are godless, immoral, unjust and unrighteous.

5. Work in the criminal justice and civil justice systems to restore righteousness and to overturn *Roe* v. *Wade*. Bring about an end to abortion. Protect the lives of all whom You have created.

6. Work in and through the governors of all fifty states and their state governments to bring about righteous, benevolent and wise government.

7. Work in all towns, villages and cities to bring about good and wise government.

8. Protect and purify all police departments, and enable them to win the war on drugs and crime. Remove those men and women who are corrupt, immoral, ungodly and racist.

9. Fund, protect and watch over fire departments throughout the land.

10. Work in the school systems and school boards to put into office those officials, administrators, and teachers who will return our schools to biblical morality and a reverence for God. Enable the gospel to penetrate the lives of our children.

11. Protect, strengthen, encourage, and give wisdom to all the leaders of the armed forces: the Army, Navy, Air Force, Marines and Coast Guard.

12. Protect and keep in righteousness those working at the Pentagon; CIA; FBI; DEA; and Bureau of Alcohol, Tobacco, and Firearms.

13. Bring about a public consensus about the desperate need to repay the national debt and to balance the budget, for no nation can survive by denying the laws of fiscal responsibility.

14. Give wisdom and Your blessing to our nation's foreign policy decisions, and keep us from war.

15. Bring about Your solution to our nation's healthcare problems.

16. Work to restore our inner cities and to redeem the people who live there from godlessness, immorality, poverty and financial debt.

17. Work in our economy to create jobs for all.

18. Provide godly solutions to the problems of homelessness, mental illness, and welfare. Remember the poor and enable the government and the Church to feed and care for them.

19. Bring about a return to biblical morality.

20. Bring about the restoration of families and the end of divorce, adultery, child abuse, domestic violence, the abandonment of children to day-care centers and peer pressure.

21. Turn people from the depravity of homosexuality, and bring repentance among all who condone it.

22. Have mercy on widows, orphans, refugees and those who are aliens in our country. Bless them through the Church and through a loving American society.

> Finally, we pray that You save many in our nation because of the worthiness of Christ, whom You gave as a ransom for all men (1 Tim. 2:3-6). We apply His completed work at the cross to the sins of unbelievers in this nation. We ask that You send out workers to bring in the harvest of salvation that You have prepared (Matt. 9:37,38). Convict sinners through the ministry of the Holy Spirit of sin, righteousness, and judgment (John 16:8). Work through every form

of media – radio, newspapers, magazines, tracts, television, movies and the Internet – to make known the gospel. Enable many more within the Church to do the work of an evangelist, and fill each with love, truth, and the Holy Spirit. Open wide the doors of opportunity for believers to share the gospel. Make believers radiant with Your love and joy as they reflect the glory of Christ (2 Cor. 3:18). Draw sinners to Your Son, for no one can come to Jesus unless You draw him (John 6:44,65). For the sake of Christ Jesus the LORD, who is worthy, we pray for the salvation of the lost from every part of this nation (Rev. 5:12).

For the sake of Your Son, Amen

PRAYER FOR THE NATIONS OF THE WORLD

Dear heavenly Father,

We do not know the nations of the world as You know them (Psa. 66:7; 99:2). We count on Your knowledge of each one and of all who live within them (Psa. 139). We ask You to forgive the sins of the nations because You have given Christ as a ransom for all men (1 Tim. 2:6). Please count as worthy the blood of Your Son, who died for the sins of the whole world (1 John 2:2). As Your priests, we ask You to forgive every sin that is the result of unbelief and rebellion against You. We claim Your promise:

> "For God so loved the world that He gave His one and only Son, that whoever believes in Him shall not perish but have eternal life. For God did not send His Son into the world to condemn the world, but to save the world through Him." (John 3:16,17)

According to Your will, we ask You for the nations of the world: "Ask of Me, and I will make the nations your inheritance, the ends of the earth your possession." (Psa. 2:8)

In obedience to Your command, we pray first for all those in authority over the nations of the world. (1 Tim. 2:1) We ask You to establish righteous government and leadership within each nation because You connect good government with the salvation of men. (1 Tim. 2:2-6) We pray that the governments You establish will be just, allow freedom of religion, provide opportunities to earn a living, feed the poor, care for widows, orphans and aliens, and provide justice and liberty. Enable the members of Your church, wherever they live, to live peaceful and quiet lives in all godliness and holiness, so that by being salt and light, the church may be Your means of bringing salvation to many. (1 Tim. 2:3) Purify the church throughout the world, and send Your workers to reap the harvest You have prepared. (Matt. 9:37,38. Open doors for the gospel in every nation, and show believers where You are at work so that they may join

You. (Col. 4:3; John 5:19,20) Revive believers so that by the love we show one another all men will know that we are Your disciples. (John 13:35) Bring us to complete unity to let the world know that You sent Jesus. (John 17:23)

We ask You to draw many within each nation to Your Son, enabling them to believe in Him. (John 6:44,65) Convict of sin, righteousness, and judgment through the ministry of the Holy Spirit by the preaching of the gospel. Make known the gospel in dreams and visions, through personal evangelism and preaching, through every kind of media (radio, TV, movies, magazines, tracts, newspapers, the Internet, and so on) and in every way possible. For who can call upon the name of the Lord if they have not heard His name (Rom. 10:14,17)? We claim Your promise that whoever does call upon the name of the Lord will be saved. (Acts 2:21)

Father, because the Scripture tells us so, we also believe that Satan has blinded the minds of unbelievers so that they cannot see the light of the gospel of the glory of Christ, who is the image of God. (2 Cor. 4:4) We ask You to have mercy on their blindness! Jesus came to proclaim freedom for the prisoners and recovery of sight for the blind, and to release the oppressed. (Luke 4:18,19) He is alive at Your right hand and lives today and forever to fulfill this same blessed ministry of deliverance! We believe Your promise that He has other sheep that are not yet of the same sheep pen; please bring them in also. Enable them to listen to the Great Shepherd's voice and to follow Him. (John 10:27,16) Make us one flock with one Shepherd. (John 10:16)

Finally, we know that You saved those who already believe, not because of any righteous things we had done, but because of Your mercy. (Titus 3:4,5) We pray that Your mercy may extend to as many as possible for the sake of the glory of Your Son, who is worthy. (Rev. 5:12)

For the glory of Christ, Amen

MAPS AND LISTS OF THE
NATIONS OF THE WORLD

On the following pages are six sets of maps and data tables encompassing all the nations of the world. Take one set per day. Mention some or all of the following subjects to the Lord in prayer then name the nations to Him one after another from each map. In this way you are applying His will to a list of nations in a short period of time. In one week you will have prayed for all the nations of the world!

Dear heavenly Father,

Please do the following in each of these nations that I will name before You this day:

1. Make these nations the inheritance of Christ, His possession. (Psa. 2:8)

2. Count as worthy the blood of Your Son for the remission of the sins of many. (1 John 2:2)

3. Establish righteous governments and leadership within these nations for the protection of Your Church and for the salvation of the lost. (1 Tim. 2:2-6)

4. Enable believers within these nations to live peaceful and quiet lives in all godliness and holiness so that by being salt and light many people may be saved. (1 Tim. 2:3)

5. Send out Your workers to reap the harvest You have prepared. (Matt. 9:37,38)

6. Revive believers within these nations so that by the love they show one another all men will know that they are Your disciples. (John 13:35)

7. Bring believers to complete unity within these nations to let unbelievers know that You sent Jesus. (John 17:23)

8. Draw men, women and children to the Lord enabling them to believe in Him. (John 6:44,65)

9. Make known the gospel of Jesus Christ in every way possible: in dreams, visions, through personal evangelism, preaching, and through every kind of media. For who can call upon the name of the Lord if they have never heard it? (Rom. 10:14,17)

10. Please take the blindness Satan has caused from the minds of unbelievers in these nations. (2 Cor. 4:4)

11. Have mercy upon the lost in every one of these nations according to Your lovingkindness, mercy, faithfulness, compassion and graciousness. (Titus 3:5; Psa. 108:4; Ex. 34:6,7)

12. Bring peace to Jerusalem and bring many Jews to their Messiah. (Psa. 122:6; Rom. 9:1,2)

13. Open the door for the message of the Gospel. Enable believers to proclaim it clearly as they should. Enable them to be wise around outsiders and to make the most of every opportunity. (Col. 4:3-6)

14. Save many people in these nations because it is Your will that all men be saved and Christ Jesus has been given as a ransom for all men. (I Tim. 2:4-6)

15. Set free from captivity all those who belong to Christ who are in prison; remind believers to pray for prisoners and to visit them until they are free. (Heb. 13:3; Matt. 25:26)

16. Have mercy upon the alien, the refugee, the widow, the poor, and the sick and raise up Your people to bless and care for them. (Psa. 35:10; 68:5; 146:9; Matt. 19:21; Gal 2:10; Matt. 25:35,36)

17. Do not allow the gates of hell to overcome Your Church. (Matt. 16:18)

The data in the following tables were adapted from *Operation World - 21st Century* by Patrick Johnstone and Jason Mandryk published by Paternoster Publishing, PO Box 300, Carlisle Cumbria CA3 0Q5 UK in 2001. This book is a wonderful resource for the Christian who wants to pray specifically for each of the nations of the world.

ABBREVIATIONS USED IN DATA TABLES

Religious groups:

X = Christian

B = Buddhist

Ch = Chinese

E = Ethnic, tradional

H = Hindu

J = Jewish

M = Muslim

N = Non-religious

Z = Other, various combined groups

Population is noted in millions, e.g. 50 = 50,000,000.

NORTH AMERICA

	Population 2000	Main Religions	non-Chr%	All Chr%	Evang-elical%	Peoples All	Unevangelized groups
Bermuda	0.1	X	6.7	93.3	19.6	6	1
Canada	31.1	X	24.3	75.7	10.8	151	1
Greenland	0.1	X	3.4	96.6	1.6	4	0
St Pierre & Miquelon	0.0	X	2.3	97.7	0.4	2	0
United States of America	278.4	X	15.5	84.5	32.5	306	22
Totals (5 countries)	309.7		18.4	81.6	30.3	469	24

AFRICA

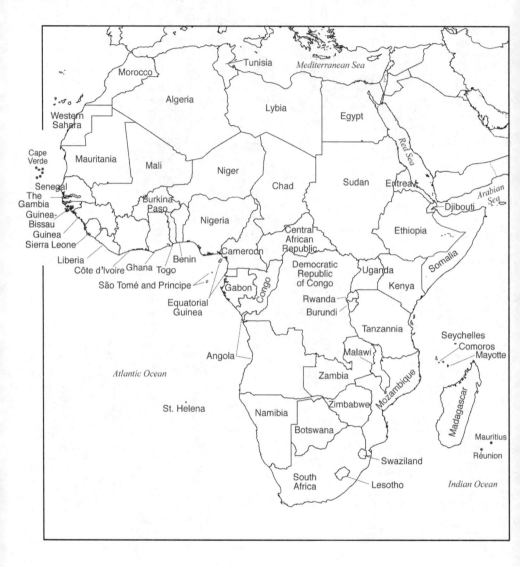

	Population 2000	Main Religions	non-Chr%	All Chr%	Evang-elical%	Peoples All	Unevangelized groups
Algeria	31.5	M	99.7	0.3	0.2	43	36
Angola	12.9	X	5.9	94.1	16.4	59	7
Benin	6.1	EXM	68.2	31.8	4.2	57	29
Botswana	1.6	XE	33.1	66.9	8.0	53	20
British Indian Ocean	0.0	na	0.0	0.0	0.0	4	0
Burkino Faso	11.9	MEX	81.6	18.4	8.0	79	61
Burundi	6.7	XE	9.9	90.1	20.0	13	3
Cameroon	15.1	XM	31.0	69.0	6.4	296	75
Cape Verde Islands	0.4	X	4.9	95.1	4.7	6	0
Central African Republic	3.6	XME	29.6	70.4	34.8	94	19
Chad	7.7	MXE	72.2	27.8	13.5	135	86
Comoros	0.6	M	99.2	0.8	0.1	10	6
Congo	2.9	X	8.7	91.3	13.8	78	2
Congo-DRC	51.7	X	4.7	95.3	19.4	259	4
Côte d'Ivoire	14.8	MXE	68.2	31.8	9.2	192	39
Djibouti	0.6	M	95.3	4.7	0.1	9	5
Egypt	68.5	M	87.0	13.0	2.5	37	21
Equatorial Guinea	0.5	X	4.9	95.1	3.2	22	2
Eritrea	3.9	MX	52.6	47.4	1.7	15	7
Ethiopia	62.6	XM	35.0	65.0	19.7	144	64
Gabon	1.2	XEM	22.1	77.9	14.2	50	2
Gambia, The	1.3	ME	95.9	4.1	0.3	31	19
Ghana	20.2	XME	36.5	63.6	14.8	107	24
Guinea	7.4	ME	95.3	4.7	1.0	43	32
Guinea-Bissau	1.2	MEX	85.7	14.3	1.1	31	23
Kenya	30.1	XEM	21.4	78.6	35.8	123	45
Lesotho	2.2	XE	28.2	71.9	8.2	12	0
Liberia	3.2	EXM	61.7	38.3	9.1	46	5
Libya	5.6	M	97.5	2.5	0.3	39	26
Madagascar	15.9	XEM	37.2	62.8	8.8	54	11
Malawi	10.9	XME	22.2	77.8	20.4	30	3
Mali	11.2	ME	98.2	1.8	0.8	44	39
Mauritania	2.7	M	99.8	0.2	0.0	25	21
Mauritius	1.2	HXM	67.1	32.9	7.9	23	1
Mayotte	0.1	M	97.1	2.9	0.0	9	7
Morocco	28.2	M	99.9	0.1	0.0	31	24
Mozambique	19.7	XEM	42.4	57.7	13.5	56	7
Namibia	1.7	XEN	20.1	80.0	10.3	32	11
Niger	10.7	M	99.6	0.4	0.1	36	24
Nigeria	111.5	XME	47.4	52.6	23.5	490	189
Réunion	0.7	XHN	15.1	84.9	5.2	16	2
Rwanda	7.7	XM	19.2	80.8	22.8	12	3
São Tomé	0.1	X	7.1	92.9	2.2	6	0
Senegal	9.5	M	95.2	4.8	0.1	57	38
Seychelles	0.1	X	3.1	96.9	5.3	9	1
Sierra Leone	4.9	MEX	88.3	11.7	3.2	30	15
Somalia	10.1	M	100.0	0.1	0.0	28	22
South Africa	40.4	XEN	26.5	73.5	19.3	69	2
St. Helena	0.0	X	4.3	95.7	5.2	3	0
Sudan	29.5	MXE	76.8	23.2	10.3	244	165
Swaziland	1.0	XE	17.3	82.7	29.4	11	1
Tanzania	33.5	XME	48.6	51.4	17.0	162	38
Togo	4.6	XEM	49.3	50.7	9.0	52	11
Tunisia	9.6	M	99.8	0.2	0.0	24	15
Uganda	21.8	XM	11.4	88.7	46.3	62	5
Western Sahara	0.3	M	0.0	0.0	0.0	11	10
Zambia	9.2	XE	15.0	85.0	25.0	85	5
Zimbabwe	11.7	XE	28.3	71.7	25.3	41	3
Total (58 countries)	784.3		51.6	48.4	14.8	3839	1335

LATIN AMERICA/CARIBBEAN

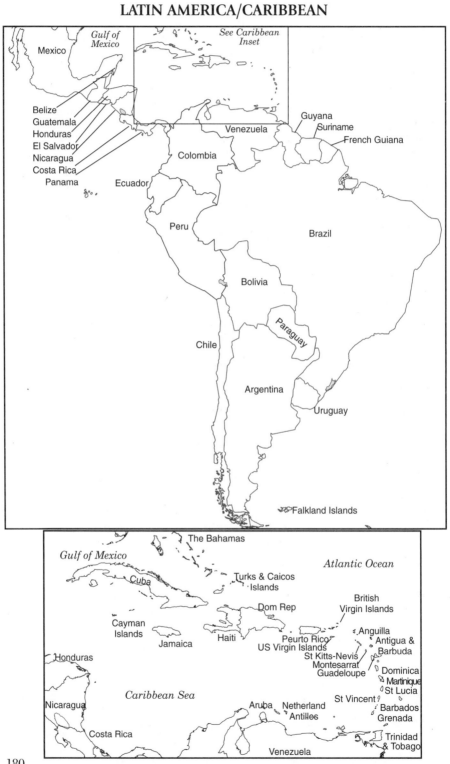

	Population 2000	Main Religions	non-Chr%	All Chr%	Evang-elical%	Peoples All	Unevangelized groups
Anguilla	0.0	X	7.5	91.5	19.9	4	0
Antigua & Barbuda	0.1	X	6.2	93.9	16.8	5	0
Argentina	37.0	X	7.9	92.9	10.8	63	1
Aruba	0.1	X	3.4	96.5	6.4	6	2
Bahamas, The	0.3	XN	7.5	92.4	30.8	8	1
Barbados	0.3	X	3.4	95.7	28.6	10	1
Belize	0.2	X	7.2	91.0	14.1	18	1
Bolivia	8.3	X	6.0	93.9	11.8	57	5
Brazil	170.3	X	11.6	91.4	12.6	223	16
British Virgin Islands	0.0	X	13.4	86.0	27.2	7	0
Cayman Islands	0.0	XEN	22.1	78.0	25.5	5	1
Chile	15.2	XN	11.6	89.2	16.8	24	1
Colombia	42.3	X	4.6	95.5	4.7	98	8
Costa Rica	4.0	X	5.1	94.7	12.4	21	1
Cuba	11.2	XNE	53.5	46.9	4.6	14	1
Dominica	0.1	X	3.5	94.9	13.5	9	0
Dominican Republic	8.5	X	6.4	95.2	7.6	13	0
Ecuador	12.6	X	2.7	97.4	6.1	32	4
El Salvador	6.3	X	2.2	97.3	21.7	14	2
Falkland Islands	0.0	X	6.0	94.3	22.7	5	0
French Guiana	0.2	XN	14.5	84.9	3.3	23	3
Grenada	0.1	X	3.7	97.0	18.0	9	0
Guadeloupe	0.5	X	5.2	94.6	5.4	6	0
Guatemala	11.4	X	2.6	97.5	26.0	64	1
Guyana	0.9	XHN	56.1	43.6	11.1	23	1
Haiti	8.2	X	4.9	95.5	22.2	8	1
Honduras	6.5	X	3.1	96.7	17.7	26	2
Jamaica	2.6	XE	16.0	84.1	26.3	13	1
Martinique	0.4	XN	8.2	91.6	5.4	8	0
Mexico	98.9	X	6.0	94.5	6.7	277	4
Montserrat	0.0	X	2.5	95.5	27.6	7	0
Netherlands Antilles	0.2	X	5.8	96.1	7.6	14	0
Nicaragua	5.1	XN	9.2	90.9	16.3	21	1
Panama	2.9	X	8.5	88.1	18.2	32	0
Paraguay	5.5	X	5.1	98.0	4.8	44	2
Peru	25.7	XN	9.8	90.1	8.7	110	15
Puerto Rico	3.9	X	3.4	97.0	27.6	11	0
St Kitts-Nevis	0.0	X	4.0	95.6	22.9	5	0
St Lucia	0.2	X	4.1	96.1	12.3	6	1
St Vincent	0.1	X	7.7	92.2	24.2	12	0
Suriname	0.4	XHM	52.3	46.9	4.1	27	4
Trinidad & Tobago	1.3	XHM	28.9	71.2	15.2	15	1
Turks & Caicos Islands	0.0	X	7.9	93.2	34.3	4	0
Uruguay	3.3	XNE	39.7	60.2	4.5	31	1
Venezuela	24.2	X	4.8	94.7	10.1	69	5
Virgin Islands of the USA	0.1	X	3.2	96.9	25.8	8	1
Totals (46 Countries)	519.1		8.3	91.7	10.6	1509	89

ASIA

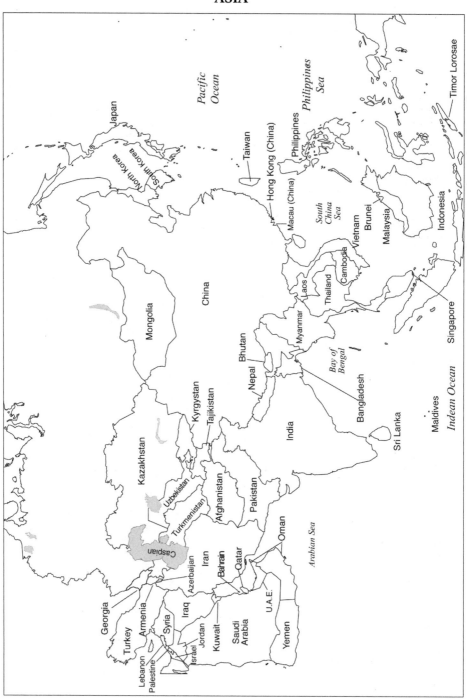

	Population 2000	Main Religions	non-Chr%	All Chr%	Evang-elical%	Peoples All	Unevangelized groups
Afghanistan	22.7	M	100.0	0.0	0.0	69	65
Armenia	3.5	XN	15.0	85.0	8.1	24	10
Azerbaijan	7.7	MN	95.4	4.6	0.1	34	22
Bahrain	0.6	MX	89.6	10.4	3.1	13	6
Bangladesh	129.2	MH	99.3	0.7	0.4	60	30
Bhutan	2.1	BH	99.5	0.5	0.4	26	24
Brunei	0.3	MXBE	88.8	11.3	4.6	26	11
Cambodia	11.2	B	98.8	1.2	0.5	36	25
China, Hong Kong	7.0	ChNX	90.0	10.1	5.1	n.a.	n.a.
China, Macau	0.4	NChBX	92.7	73.	1.7	n.a.	n.a.
China, People's Republic	1262.6	NChBX	92.8	7.3	6.0	476	187
China, Taiwan	22.4	ChNBX	9.39	6.1	2.7	29	6
Georgia	5.0	XMN	37.5	62.5	1.4	34	17
India	1013.7	HM	93.7	6.3	1.8	438	308
Indonesia	213.0	MX	84.0	16.0	40.0	743	284
Iran	67.7	M	99.7	0.3	0.0	77	65
Iraq	23.1	M	98.5	1.6	0.1	35	22
Israel	5.1	JM	97.8	2.3	0.2	52	29
Japan	126.7	BZ	98.4	1.6	0.4	33	18
Jordan	6.7	M	97.3	2.8	0.2	19	9
Kazakhstan	16.2	MXN	75.3	24.7	0.6	48	25
Korea, North	24.0	NEZ	98.3	1.7	1.5	6	3
Korea, South	46.8	NXBE	68.3	31.7	15.5	8	1
Kuwait	2.0	MX	91.8	8.2	0.6	26	8
Kyrgyzstan	4.7	MNX	92.2	7.8	0.6	41	24
Laos	534	BE	98.2	1.9	1.2	96	82
Lebanon	3.3	MXZ	68.1	31.9	0.6	18	3
Malaysia	22.2	MChXH	90.8	9.2	4.1	173	95
Maldives	0.3	M	99.9	0.1	0.0	8	5
Mongolia	2.7	NEB	99.3	0.7	0.5	20	18
Myanmar	45.6	BX	91.3	8.7	5.2	132	63
Nepal	23.9	HBM	98.1	1.9	1.6	117	100
Oman	2.5	M	97.5	2.5	0.3	25	13
Pakistan	156.5	M	97.7	2.3	0.4	92	80
Palestine Authority	3.4	MJ	98.1	1.9	0.1	20	5
Philipines	76.0	XM	6.8	93.2	16.7	182	91
Qatar	0.6	MXH	89.5	10.5	2.5	20	9
Saudi Arabia	21.6	M	95.5	4.5	0.9	38	18
Singapore	3.6	BMNXCh	85.4	14.6	7.8	46	9
Sri Lanka	18.8	BHMX	92.4	7.6	1.3	21	9
Syria	16.1	MX	94.9	5.1	0.1	27	8
Tajikistan	6.2	MN	98.6	1.4	0.1	40	23
Thailand	61.4	BM	98.4	1.6	0.7	94	52
Timore Lorosae	0.9	XE	10.8	89.2	2.5	21	1
Turkey	66.6	M	99.7	0.3	0.0	56	36
Turkmenistan	4.5	MN	97.3	2.7	0.0	37	21
United Arab Emirates	2.4	MHX	90.8	9.3	0.8	38	18
Uzbekistan	24.3	MN	98.7	1.3	0.3	63	35
Vietnam	79.8	BNXEZ	91.8	8.2	1.4	99	52
Yemen	18.1	M	100.0	0.1	0.0	21	11
Total (50 countries)	3692		91.4	8.6	3.6	3548	1862

EUROPE

This includes all countries of Europe and the entire Russian Federation (including all of Siberia which is technically in Asia). Cyprus is also included in Europe since it is likely to join the European Union.

	Population 2000	Main Religions	non-Chr%	All Chr%	Evang-elical%	Peoples All	Unevangelized groups
Albania	3.1	XMN	58.5	41.5	0.3	11	4
Andorra	0.1	XN	6.6	93.4	0.2	10	3
Austria	8.2	X	10.2	89.8	0.5	35	3
Belarus	10.2	XN	21.3	78.7	1.5	25	6
Belgium	10.2	XN	32.3	67.7	0.7	25	7
Bosnia	4.0	MX	65.0	35.0	0.07	19	3
Bulgaria	8.2	XMN	19.8	80.2	2	34	6
Channel Islands	0.2	XN	15.1	84.9	0	5	0
Croatia	4.5	X	5.6	94.4	0.5	30	5
Cyprus	0.8	XM	25.9	74.1	0.2	9	2
Czech Republic	10.2	XN	46.8	53.2	1.1	25	1
Denmark	5.3	XN	14.2	85.9	4.8	28	2
Estonia	1.4	NX	61.4	38.6	5.7	23	4
Faeroe Islands	0.0	XN	6.0	94.0	28.5	4	0
Finland	5.2	XN	12.9	87.1	12.5	30	7
France	59.1	XNM	32.3	67.7	0.8	96	12
Germany	82.2	XN	30.5	69.5	2.9	78	4
Gibraltar	0.0	XM	11.6	88.4	1.4	6	0
Greece	10.6	X	4.9	95.2	0.4	30	4
Holy See (Vatican)	0.0	X	0.0	100.0	0	3	0
Hungary	10.0	XN	8.0	92.0	2.7	22	2
Iceland	0.3	X	4.4	95.6	3.3	9	0
Ireland	3.7	X	4.7	95.4	3.3	20	1
Isle of Man	0.1	XN	11.2	88.8	0	4	0
Italy	57.3	XN	22.7	77.4	0.9	59	4
Latvia	2.4	XN	41.8	58.3	7.6	34	8
Liechtenstein	0.0	XN	11.3	88.7	0.4	5	1
Lithuania	3.7	XN	23.8	76.2	0.4	23	7
Luxembourg	0.4	X	6.1	93.9	0.3	14	1
Macedonia	2.0	XMN	36.6	63.4	0.2	23	3
Malta	0.4	X	2.8	97.2	1	10	0
Moldova	4.4	X	4.6	95.4	3.3	31	10
Monaco	0.0	XN	12.3	87.7	1	14	1
Netherlands	15.8	XNM	44.1	55.9	4.5	45	3
Norway	4.5	XN	6.3	93.7	9.3	31	3
Poland	38.8	XN	9.7	90.3	0.2	23	4
Portugal	9.9	XN	5.6	94.4	3.1	29	1
Romania	22.3	XN	12.2	87.9	6.3	28	6
Russia	146.9	XNM	45.9	54.1	0.7	168	83
San Marino	0.0	XN	7.7	92.7	0	3	0
Slovakia	5.4	XN	17.1	92.9	1.5	18	1
Slovenia	2.0	XN	14.8	85.2	0.2	14	0
Spain	39.8	XN	32.2	67.8	0.4	35	3
Svalbard	0.0	XN	47.0	57.0	0	2	0
Sweden	8.9	XN	45.4	54.7	4.9	50	5
Switzerland	7.4	XN	13.4	86.6	4.1	38	4
Ukraine	50.5	XN	11.9	88.1	2.7	65	23
United Kingdom	58.8	XN	32.4	67.6	8.5	94	9
Yugoslavia	10.6	XMN	32.1	67.9	1.4	34	4
Total (49 countries)	737.5					1491	283

PACIFIC

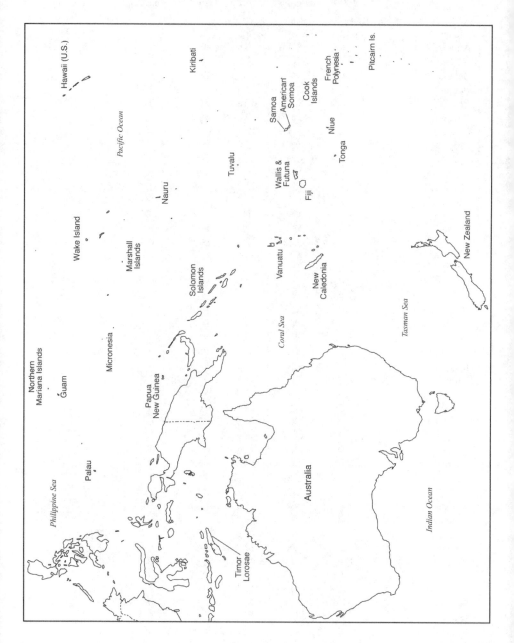

	Population 2000	Main Religions	non-Chr%	All Chr%	Evang-elical%	Peoples All	Unevangelized groups
American Samoa	0.1	X	4.3	95.7	17.9	9	1
Australia	18.9	XN	32.5	67.5	12.5	132	16
Christmas Island	0.0	MNX	87.0	13.0	0.0	7	3
Cocos (Keeling) Is.	0.0	MXN	63.0	37.0	0.0	4	2
Cook Islands	0.0	X	2.0	98.0	12.1	7	0
Fiji	0.8	XHM	41.7	58.3	17.5	29	1
French Polynesia	0.2	XN	15.0	85.1	5.6	14	0
Guam	0.2	X	4.4	95.6	12.6	12	1
Johnston Island	0.0	X	30.0	70.0	0.0		
Kiribati	0.1	XE	5.6	94.4	7.0	5	0
Marshall Islands	0.1	X	4.8	96.2	42.8	2	0
Micronesia, Fed. States	0.1	X	2	93.3	21.5	21	0
Midway Islands	0.0		0.0	0.0	0.0		
Nauru	0.0	X	9.5	90.5	9.0	8	0
New Caledonia	0.2	XN	17.2	82.8	7.5	48	0
New Zealand	3.9	XN	38.3	61.7	22.1	47	0
Niue	0.0	X	5.1	94.9	8.5	3	0
Norfolk Island	0.0	XN	25.0	75.0	0.0	5	3
Northern Mariana Is.	0.1	XCH	9.5	90.5	10.4	9	0
Palau	0.0	X	3.9	96.1	21.1	4	0
Papua New Guinea	4.8	X	2.7	97.3	21.1	861	26
Pitcairn Islands	0.0	X	0.0	100.0	0.0	2	0
Samoa	0.2	X	3.1	96.9	4.0	7	0
Solomon Islands	0.4	X	3.8	96.2	34.6	75	0
Tokelau Islands	0.0	X	1.0	99.0	3.7	2	0
Tonga	0.1	X	4.8	95.2	21.6	9	0
Tuvalu	0.0	X	2.0	98.0	5.1	6	0
Vanuatu	0.2	X	8.9	91.1	31.7	122	1
Wallis & Futuna Islands	0.0	X	2.2	97.8	0.6	8	0
Totals (29 countries)	31.3		26.7	73.3	15.2	1238	31

AS YOU CONCLUDE...

Congratulations on finishing this book! What do you think? Is it not amazing the breadth and depth of prayers that God invites us to pray? Did you hear Him speaking to you as you used this book? Did you see the vision of prayer extended to you from His heart to yours? Did your heart thrill as you accepted His invitation to you personally to partner with Him in advancing His Kingdom? Did He open the eyes of your heart to "see" the lost all over this world and to care deeply for their salvation, even as Jesus does? And for your brothers and sisters all over the world, were you not burdened by the Holy Spirit for them to be strengthened by Him in the inner man that they, together with you, would please Jesus in everyway?

It may be that you were most moved by the Praise Section, as you heard from God through His Words just how great He is and how fully He has provided for you through Jesus Christ. You may have understood for the first time that He has made you a new creation—the old is gone, the new has come! And as you praised Him for the personal ways He is working in your life, you may have realized just how much He loves you and how intimately He is concerned with every detail in your life. What an amazing God you serve and how completely He is "for you"!

Or perhaps it is the Confession of Sin section that has grabbed your attention the most! You may be feeling a sense of your own sin as you never have before. Things that you didn't even realize were sin are now becoming sin to you as the Holy Spirit takes the Word of God and convicts you deeply of all that doesn't please God. Take heart! This is God's work in you to separate you from the flesh and the world so that He might fill you more fully with Himself. It can be painful to go through a time of pruning but God promises you that this is in order that you might bear much fruit.

For some of you, it is praying for believers that has moved you the most and you have a deep sense of partnership with God as you pray His will into the lives of your family, pastors, church members and ministries, and out into the world on behalf of the Church in every nation. You may be experiencing a great sense of peace as you realize you don't need to know "personal" prayer requests to pray for other believers because you are able to pray God's will and purposes into their lives always! His will for believers is the same today, yesterday, and forever—to become like Christ, to love one another deeply, to hold fast to the gospel, to edify one another with the various gifts He has given us, to do the works of service that build up the church, and to be united in the faith and in the knowledge of Jesus Christ until we all reach fullness in Him.

Or perhaps your heart sings with joy as you use the Praying for the Lost section and take a hold of His will for the lost that none might perish! You may realize for the first time that you don't need to "twist" God's arm as you pray for the salvation of your loved ones because you now see that the Scriptures promise that God wants all men to be saved and to come to knowledge of the truth! How wonderful it is to ask God in faith to do what only He can do—regenerate their hearts so that they might transfer trust from themselves to the Son of God, believing in Christ alone for salvation. I hope that you have dozens of names of unbelievers on your "List of the Lost"! If God wants them saved and you are asking for them to be saved, will not God save them? Does this truth not give you the determination to keep praying faithfully until they are? Charles Mueller, a wonderful Christian of the late eighteen hundreds and early nineteen hundreds who ran several orphanages by faith alone, prayed for thirty five years for a friend of his to be saved. On the day of Mueller's funeral, this friend for whom he had prayed most of his life came to Christ! May this story encourage you to keep on praying for each person on your list until they are saved.

FINAL ENCOURAGEMENT

Keep on praying with this book! Without a systematic way of praying, you will fail to pray as extensively and persistently as you could. This book only helps you to bear fruit for God if you use it! It won't help you partner with God in advancing His Kingdom if you leave it on a shelf.

Don't be deceived by your enemy, the devil, who hates prayer more than anything you do for the Lord because prayer is the means by which you intimately communicate with God, receiving His life as your own and giving His life to others. Think of it in this way: in prayer you do the "asking" and God does the "doing"! Is it not true that unless He does the doing that what is done isn't eternal? Only God can bring someone to Christ. Only God can change a heart. Only God can transform you into the image of Jesus. Only God can give you His love for the unlovely. Only God can forgive you your sins. And so on... If prayer doesn't under gird everything you do than all you will have is exactly that: what *you* have done but not what *God* has done!

Prayer is the pulse of your Christian life because it reveals your heart's response to God. Jesus Christ came to restore you to dependence upon Him so that you would live in Him. God wants us to pray because He knows that in Him alone is life, love, health, joy, wisdom, righteousness, power, and salvation. Jesus said, "Now this is eternal life: that they may know You, the only true God, and Jesus Christ, whom You have sent." (John 17:3) The life that we live must be His life received through prayer and given to others through prayer!

MY PRAYER FOR US ALL

Dearest Father,

I pray that out of Your glorious riches of love and power that You will fill us with the desire and ability to grow in depth, insight, and frequency of prayer. Work in us through the ministry of the Holy Spirit that we would become faithful, persistent, and complete in prayer making it the foundation of our lives. Enable us to bear much eternal fruit for Jesus Christ to the praise of His glorious grace. Burden us with Your burdens and give us Your vision of the power of prayer through which You will save the lost and build up your Church. By Your grace and mercy, enable us to become Jesus Christ's prayer partner, praying on earth as He is praying in heaven.

In Christ's Name and for His glory,
Kathie Grant

GOD'S WILL CONCERNING PRAYER

1. Devote yourselves to prayer, being watchful and thankful. (Col. 4:2)
2. Pray continually. (1Th. 5:17)
3. And pray in the Spirit on all occasions with all kinds of prayers and requests. With this in mind, be alert and always keep on praying for all the saints. (Eph. 6:18)
4. Then Jesus told His disciples a parable to show them that they should always pray and not give up. (Luke 18:1)
5. I want men everywhere to lift up holy hands in prayer, without anger or disputing. (1Tim. 2:8)
6. But when you pray, go into your room, close the door and pray to your Father, who is unseen. Then your Father, who sees what is done in secret, will reward you. (Matt. 6:6)
7. I urge, then, first of all, that requests, prayers, intercession and thanksgiving be made for everyone — for kings and all those in authority, that we may live peaceful and quiet lives in all godliness and holiness. This is good, and pleases God our Savior, who wants all men to be saved and to come to a knowledge of the truth. (1Tim. 2:1-4)
8. Do not be anxious about anything, but in everything, by prayer and petition, with thanksgiving, present your requests to God. (Phil. 4:6)
9. Is any one of you in trouble? He should pray. Is anyone happy? Let him sing songs of praise. (James 5:13)
10. Therefore confess your sins to each other and pray for each other so that you may be healed. The prayer of a righteous man is powerful and effective. (James 5:16)
11. Pray for those who persecute you, (Matt. 5:44)
12. Ask of Me, and I will make the nations your inheritance, the ends of the earth your possession. (Psa. 2:8)
13. Be...faithful in prayer. (Rom. 12:12)
14. Watch and pray so that you will not fall into temptation. (Mark 14:38)
15. And this is my prayer: that your love may abound more and more in knowledge and depth of insight. (Phil. 1:9)
16. Pray for the peace of Jerusalem: "May those who love you be secure. May there be peace within your walls and security within your citadels." (Psa. 122:6-7)

17. As for me, far be it from me that I should sin against the Lord by failing to pray for you. (1 Sam. 12:23)

18. If My people, who are called by My name, will humble themselves and pray and seek My face and turn from their wicked ways, then will I hear from heaven and will forgive their sin and will heal their land. (2 Chr. 7:14)

19. I pray also that the eyes of your heart may be enlightened in order that you may know the hope to which He has called you, the riches of His glorious inheritance in the saints, and His incomparably great power for us who believe. That power is like the working of His mighty strength. (Eph. 1:19)

20. Pray in the Holy Spirit. (Jude 1:20)

21. Be clear minded and self-controlled so that you can pray. (1 Pet. 4:7)

22. With this in mind, we constantly pray for you, that our God may count you worthy of His calling, and that by His power He may fulfill every good purpose of yours and every act prompted by your faith. (2 Th. 1:11)

23. And pray for us, too, that God may open a door for our message,...Pray that I may proclaim it clearly, as I should. (Col. 4:3-4)

24. And we pray this in order that you may live a life worthy of the Lord and may please Him in every way. (Col. 1:10)

25. We have not stopped praying for you and asking God to fill you with the knowledge of His will through all spiritual wisdom and understanding. (Col. 1:9)

26. Through Jesus, therefore, let us continually offer to God a sacrifice of praise — the fruit of lips that confess His name. (Heb. 13:15)

27. I pray that out of His glorious riches He may strengthen you with power through His Spirit in your inner being, so that Christ may dwell in your hearts through faith. (Eph. 3:17)

28. And I pray that you, being rooted and established in love, may have power, together with all the saints, to grasp how wide and long and high and deep is the love of Christ, and to know this love that surpasses knowledge — that you may be filled to the measure of all the fullness of God. (Eph. 3:17-19)

29. Sing psalms, hymns and spiritual songs with gratitude in your hearts to God. (Col. 3:16)

30. Therefore let everyone who is godly pray to You while You may be found. (Psa. 32:6)
31. And when you pray, do not keep on babbling like pagans, for they think they will be heard because of their many words. Do not be like them, for your Father knows what you need before you ask Him. (Matt. 6:7-8)
32. Praise the Lord. Praise God in His sanctuary; praise Him in His mighty heavens. Praise Him for His acts of power; praise Him for His surpassing greatness. Let everything that has breath praise the Lord. Praise the Lord. (Psa. 150:1,2,6)
33. Then I acknowledged my sin to You and did not cover up my iniquity. I said, "I will confess my transgressions to the Lord" — and You forgave the guilt of my sin. Selah. (Psa. 32:5)
34. If we confess our sins, He is faithful and just and will forgive us our sins and purify us from all unrighteousness. (1 John 1:9)
35. Then He said to His disciples, "The harvest is plentiful but the workers are few. Ask the Lord of the harvest, therefore, to send out workers into His harvest field." (Matt. 9:37-38)

THE CONDITIONS AND PROMISES FOR ANSWERED PRAYER

1. Until now you have not asked for anything in My name. Ask and you will receive, and your joy will be complete. (John 16:24)
2. And I will do whatever you ask in My name, so that the Son may bring glory to the Father. You may ask Me for anything in My name, and I will do it. (John 14:13,14)
3. If you remain in Me and My words remain in you, ask whatever you wish, and it will be given you. (John 15:7)
4. You did not choose Me, but I chose you and appointed you to go and bear fruit — fruit that will last. Then the Father will give you whatever you ask in My name. (John 15:16)
5. This is the confidence we have in approaching God: that if we ask anything according to His will, He hears us. And if we know that He hears us — whatever we ask — we know that we have what we asked of Him. (1 John 5:14-15)

6. Come near to God and He will come near to you. (James 4:8)
7. Dear friends, if our hearts do not condemn us, we have confidence before God and receive from Him anything we ask, because we obey His commands and do what pleases Him. (1 John 3:21-22)
8. "Ask and it will be given to you; seek and you will find; knock and the door will be opened to you. For everyone who asks receives; he who seeks finds; and to him who knocks, the door will be opened. (Matt. 7:7,8)
9. In the same way, the Spirit helps us in our weakness. We do not know what we ought to pray for, but the Spirit Himself intercedes for us with groans that words cannot express. And He who searches our hearts knows the mind of the Spirit, because the Spirit intercedes for the saints in accordance with God's will. (Rom. 8:26,27)
10. Do not be anxious about anything, but in everything, by prayer and petition, with thanksgiving, present your requests to God. And the peace of God, which transcends all understanding, will guard your hearts and your minds in Christ Jesus. (Phil. 4:6,7)
11. Now to Him who is able to do immeasurably more than all we ask or imagine. (Eph. 3:20)
12. And the Lord said to Moses, "I will do the very thing you have asked, because I am pleased with you and I know you by name." (Ex. 33:17)
13. You hear, O Lord, the desire of the afflicted; You encourage them, and You listen to their cry. (Psa. 10:17)
14. What the wicked dreads will overtake him; what the righteous desire will be granted. (Prov. 10:24)
15. The Lord is far from the wicked but He hears the prayer of the righteous. (Prov. 15:29)
16. Before they call I will answer; while they are still speaking I will hear. (Isa. 65:24)
17. But when you pray, go into your room, close the door and pray to your Father, who is unseen. Then your Father, who sees what is done in secret, will reward you. (Matt. 6:6)
18. Again, I tell you that if two of you on earth agree about anything you ask for, it will be done for you by My Father in heaven. For where two or three come together in My name, there am I with them. (Matt. 18:19,20)

19. If you believe, you will receive whatever you ask for in prayer. (Matt. 21:22)

20. Therefore I tell you, whatever you ask for in prayer, believe that you have received it, and it will be yours. And when you stand praying, if you hold anything against anyone, forgive him, so that your Father in heaven may forgive you your sins. (Mark 11:24,25)

21. If you then, though you are evil, know how to give good gifts to your children, how much more will your Father in heaven give the Holy Spirit to those who ask Him! (Luke 11:13)

22. And will not God bring about justice for His chosen ones, who cry out to him day and night? Will He keep putting them off? I tell you, He will see that they get justice, and quickly. (Luke 18:7,8)

23. Let us then approach the throne of grace with confidence, so that we may receive mercy and find grace to help us in our time of need. (Heb. 4:16)

24. If any of you lacks wisdom, he should ask God, who gives generously to all without finding fault, and it will be given to him. But when he asks, he must believe and not doubt, because he who doubts is like a wave of the sea, blown and tossed by the wind. That man should not think he will receive anything from the Lord. (James 1:5-7)

25. Those who know Your name will trust in You, for You, Lord, have never forsaken those who seek You. (Psa. 9:10)

26. For He who avenges blood remembers; He does not ignore the cry of the afflicted. (Psa. 9:12)

27. The righteous cry out, and the Lord hears them; He delivers them from all their troubles. (Psa. 34:17)

28. Delight yourself in the Lord and He will give you the desires of your heart. (Psa. 37:4)

29. He will respond to the prayer of the destitute; He will not despise their plea. (Psa. 102:17)

30. And everyone who calls on the name of the Lord will be saved. (Joel 2:32)

31. Ask the Lord for rain in the springtime; it is the Lord who makes the storm clouds. He gives showers of rain to men, and plants of the field to everyone. (Zech. 10:1)

32. If My people, who are called by My name, will humble themselves

and pray and seek My face and turn from their wicked ways, then will I hear from heaven and will forgive their sin and will heal their land. (2 Chr. 7:14)

33. The Lord is near to all who call on Him, to all who call on Him in truth. He fulfills the desires of those who fear Him; He hears their cry and saves them. (Psa. 145:18,19)

34. In all your ways acknowledge Him, and He will make your paths straight. (Prov. 3:6)

35. Call to Me and I will answer you and tell you great and unsearchable things you do not know. (Jer. 33:3)

36. We know that God does not listen to sinners. He listens to the godly man who does his will. (John 9:31)

37. And without faith it is impossible to please God, because anyone who comes to Him must believe that He exists and that He rewards those who earnestly seek Him. (Heb. 11:6)

38. Humble yourselves before the Lord, and He will lift you up. (James 4:10)

39. Therefore confess your sins to each other and pray for each other so that you may be healed. The prayer of a righteous man is powerful and effective. (James 5:16)

40. He who conceals his sins does not prosper, but whoever confesses and renounces them finds mercy. (Prov. 28:13)

41. Then I acknowledged my sin to You and did not cover up my iniquity. I said, "I will confess my transgressions to the Lord" — and You forgave the guilt of my sin. Selah. (Psa. 32:5)

THE RESULTS

1. The Word of God will sanctify you (set you apart) for God's use. (John 17:17)

2. You will be brought into the very presence of God to know and enjoy Him. (Jer. 9:24; John 14:21)

3. You will be convicted of sin and set free from it. (John 16:8; 17:17)

4. You will be brought to complete surrender to God through Christ and be counted as worthy by God to have your prayers answered. (Prov. 15:8; Matt. 21:22; 1 Peter 3:12,15a; Rom. 12:1; James 5:16b)

5. You will fulfill the role of a priest according to the will of God. (Rev. 5:10; 1 Tim. 2:1–6; 1 Peter 2:5, 9)
6. You will maximize the fruit that you bear and bring the most glory to God. (John 15:7,8,16; 16:23; Col. 1:10)
7. You may well indeed become God's partner in bringing about the greatest revival the world has ever known, to prepare the Bride for her Bridegroom, our precious Lord Jesus. (Deut. 4:29; 2 Chr. 7:14; 15:2)

"AMEN. COME, LORD JESUS." (Rev. 22:20)

PRAYER PARTNERS WITH GOD

ABOUT THE AUTHOR

Kathie came to Christ at age thirty, having searched for Him all of her life. She had experienced the poverty and hopelessness of living without a personal relationship with Jesus Christ. Her twin, sister, Christina Free, witnessed to her and prayed for her for six years without seemingly any breakthrough.

Then in March of 1978, Kathie called her brother, Andrew Free, and poured out her heart to him expressing her profound emotional despair. He listened with a love she had never experienced before. At the end of the hour and a half call, he said, "Kathie, I know that Jesus Christ died for you that you would not have to suffer this way!" She got off the phone, sank to the floor, and wept as she had never wept before. She cried out to God, "If you are the true God who loves me, please reveal yourself to me!" She knew that God would have to enable her to know Him for she couldn't reach Him without His enablement.

Two months later, she received a large envelope from the postman for which she had to pay extra postage. When she opened it, she discovered a seventy-nine page, handwritten letter from Andrew. It had taken him two months to write everything he could think of to convince her that Jesus Christ is the God who loves her, who died for her on the cross, who was raised again, who sits at the right hand of the Father, and who lives forever to be her Savior and Lord!

Kathie said to God, "How could anyone love me this much?" For the first time in her life, she heard from God when He spoke to her and said, "I have loved you with an everlasting love." Trembling with awe, she immediately gave her life to the Lord. She told Him, "I will follow You all the days of my life—don't You ever let me betray You!" Having lived with impotence all her life, she knew that only the grace of God would keep her from falling away.

The next morning, she awoke with the strong determination to call Andrew to have him pray with her to receive Jesus Christ as her Savior and Lord. When she called him, he had left town on vacation! She got off the phone and thought, "I know only two other Christians in the world: President Jimmy Carter and Christina." She didn't think she could get through

198

to President Carter, so at 9:30 in the morning she called Christina who was in the hospital about to have foot surgery. Christina acted as cool as a cucumber even though the week before she had told her pastor in Arlington, VA, that "Kathie was too hard of a nut to crack"!

They prayed together and Kathie gave her life to Christ forever, asking Him not only to save her from the penalty of her sins but to save her from the power of sin in the future. She asked Him to make her a new person and to enable her to live a life that pleased Him. For the next four hours, she was unable to move and experienced a spiritual warfare around her body. Then God, the Holy Spirit, rushed into her body and filled her from the top of her head to the soles of her feet!

Immediately, she jumped up, ran to her car, drove to a book store and bought her first Bible! She started reading the Bible that day and continued for the next four days until she had read through the entire New Testament. When she was finished, she was overcome with terror, for she was certain that she would never be able to live up to what God wanted of her. She was tempted to "edit" the Bible—to believe and obey this verse but not the other one that seemed too hard. Then the Lord brought to her mind His own words, "Heaven and earth will pass away, but my words will never pass away." (Matt. 24:35) Her response to this verse was to make a commitment to seek with all her heart to believe and obey every word of the Holy Bible.

The next day, as she was burdened in prayer to the point of anguish for sinners all over the world who do not know Jesus, the Lord gave her a picture which became His "call" to her to become an intercessor. The world was laid out like a flat oval disk, and was covered in darkness. She could see sinners drowning in their sins and hear them groaning in despair. She cried out to God, "What must they do?"

She saw herself as she had been before her own salvation, just like each of them. She saw herself turn to God—and the light of Jesus fell upon her like a beam of pure joy. All her sins slid off her body to the ground and she was clean! She saw Jesus standing on the edge of history, weeping. When she asked Him why He was crying, He said,—"They don't know that I love them! Pray that they will know my love."

Then Kathie was inside the Lord praying for the lost and for revival for the Church. She saw the world like a globe, and, in answer to her prayers, the blood of Jesus came down for the remission of sins. Next, she saw the Holy Spirit come down upon the whole earth, like gold, bringing the greatest revival the world has ever seen.

But Kathie did not rest with this vision! She obeyed this personal "call" from God to drive her to the Scriptures. For seventeen years she searched the Scriptures to discover the will of God in prayer and to meet His conditions and claim His promises for answered prayer. She called the United Nations during the first week of her salvation to get a list of all the nations of the world and began to pray systematically, comprehensively, and Scripturally for the Church and for the salvation of the lost worldwide.

Her husband, Paul, grew up in a Jewish home and was brought to his Messiah primarily by the changes he saw in Kathie, by the love he received from Kathie's new Christian friends, and by the conversations he had with Pastor Ray Dupont and Pastor Paul Jensen. He read through the New Testament, many of the prophecies in the Old Testament, and *Christianity Is Jewish* by Edith Schafer. On his thirty-fifth birthday on July 12, 1978, he gave his life to the Messiah, Jesus Christ.

Over the years that followed, Paul's life was changed in everyway. He practiced dermatology in a solo practice for nineteen years and shared the gospel regularly with his patients. His staff was the wives of Denver Seminary students and was partners with him in seeking to impact his patients with the good news of Jesus Christ. He studied Evangelism Explosion, a wonderful program that teaches how to share one's faith, became a deacon in his local church, and was the leader of many Bible studies. In 1986, he started the Bread of Life Foundation, dedicated to the furtherance of the gospel, from some of the proceeds of royalties he received for his invention of Rogaine, a drug that grows hair. From 1995 to 1997, he attended Denver Seminary and graduated with a Certificate of Theology. He served on the Board of Directors of Promise Keepers from 1999 to 2002.

Armed with Paul's degree and Kathie's years of experience in prayer, in 1995 they began to teach Christians how to pray in the Word of God for the panoramic scope of prayer commanded by the Lord in the Bible. Together they have taught thousands of Christians in eighteen denominations and nineteen states the power of Scriptural praying. Kathie can be heard daily on her national radio show, "Let's Pray."

Prayer Seminars, Radio Ministry and Ordering Books

How is your church doing in prayer? Fifty percent of Christians are praying only three to five minutes a day! Even though almost all Christians rate prayer as being a "10" in importance in living the Christian life, they rate their own prayer life a "4" and think that God would rate it a "3". In a survey of thousands of Christians by the Institute for Church Development, sixty percent wanted help from their pastor to develop a greater consistency in their personal prayer time during the middle of the week.

Help is available! Kathie Grant and her husband, Dr. Paul Grant, a physician, the inventor of Rogaine, and a graduate of Denver Seminary, are eager to come to your church to inspire, teach, and equip your people to pray. They have spoken to thousands of Christians in nineteen different denominations in nineteen states the power of Scriptural praying. Their teaching is Biblical and inspirational.

These are the names of the denominations and groups they have taught to pray the Word of God: American Baptist Churches in the U.S.A., Assemblies of God, Free Methodist, Southern Baptist Convention, Baptist Missionary Association of America, Berean Fundamental Church, United Methodist Church, Evangelical Free Church, Jewish Christian, Church of God Seventh Day, Christian Church, Evangelical Presbyterian Church, Cumberland Presbyterian Church, Christian Reformed in North America, Church of the Brethren, Worldwide Church of God, Interdenominational, Community Churches, Nazarene, Women's Aglow, The Fellowship of Christian Athletes, The Christian Legal Society and Marriage Watchers.

How It Works

When you invite them to come to your church to give a prayer seminar, they will first ask your pastor to give the congregation a forty question prayer survey that evaluates the practice of prayer in their lives. They arrive on Saturday afternoon and present your pastor with a 40 page survey report that goes into detail about the prayer habits of his people. On Sunday morning, either during the sermon time or in a ten-minute promo, they present an inspirational message that convicts, inspires, and excites people to come back to church that evening for a two hour prayer seminar.

The prayer seminar opens with a discussion of the results of the prayer survey, moves on to a solid, Biblical teaching of God's commands, conditions, and promises of answered prayer (interspersed with inspirational stories), and then presents this book as a way to please the Lord in prayer.

CHANGED PRAYER LIVES

The following are just two of the responses the Grants have received after giving their prayer seminar; others are available upon request as well as the names, addresses, and phone numbers of the pastors of the churches where they have spoken:

"I can't thank you enough for challenging our church to a more zealous and intentional prayer life. Even months after the seminar, people continue to pray the Scriptures and tell me of the tremendous work God is doing among us as a result. Your seminar ignited a spark of fervent prayer in our congregation that is bearing significant and eternal fruit. May God be praised!"

Pastor Larry Orth,
Calvary Church, Rochester, MN

"Every feedback I have received and every comment I have heard, without exception, has suggested that your presentation was exactly what our people wanted to hear! Your teaching on prayer laid a wonderful Scriptural foundation for the entire seminar and your concluding presentation, which walked us through the book, provided the structure, guidance, and direction that so many people were looking for.

In addition to the content, you two work so well together that you wonderfully model your love for the Lord and for one another in ways that are both encouraging and inviting to those who see and hear you. In fact, so powerfully were you used of God that I have heard some say that their prayer lives will never be the same.

Though "thank you" seems inadequate to convey how appreciative we are as a church, please know that you two were used of God in extraordinary ways and we truly rejoice in your servant's hearts, in your willingness to give so completely of yourselves, and in the passion for prayer that is so evident to all."

Pastor Bret Truax,
Crossroads Baptist Church, Northgenn, CO

How to Contact the Grants to Schedule a Prayer Seminar

Call **Prayer Partners With God** toll-free at (877) 267-2445 (outside of Colorado) or (303) 781-6484 or fax (303) 781-6585. Or you can learn more through their website PrayerPartnersWithGod.com, or by writing them at Prayer Partners With God, P.O. Box 9292, Englewood, CO 80111.

How to Order Additional Books

For additional copies of this book the prices are as follows:

1-5 copies is $15.00 each
6-9 copies is $12.00 each
10-15 is $11.00 each
Volume discounts are available

Please make checks payable to **Prayer Partners With God Publishing**. Shipping and handling are included in these prices. (For priority mail, please add $2.00 per book to the above prices.)

Books may be ordered in the following ways:

- Use the order form on the following page
- Order from our secure website at
  PrayerPartnersWithGod.com (credit cards accepted)
- Call us at (303) 781-6484 or
  1-877-267-2445 (toll-free outside Colorado)
- Fax us at (303) 781-6585
- Mail us at Prayer Partners With God
  P.O. Box 9292
  Englewood, CO 80111

WE NEED YOUR STORIES OF ANSWERED PRAYER!

We are looking for inspirational stories of answered prayers to share with listeners on our national daily radio show, "Let's Pray!" and in our prayer seminars. Please contact us by phone at (303) 781-6484, 1-877-267-2445 (toll-fee outside Colorado), by fax at (303) 781-6585, through our website at PrayerPartnersWithGod.com, or by mail at Prayer Partners With God Publishing, P.O. Box 9292, Englewood, CO 80111. We reserve the right to choose which stories are used.

Book Order Form

The prices for copies of this book are as follows:

> 1-5 copies is $15.00 each
> 6-9 copies is $12.00 each
> 10-15 is $11.00 each
> Volume discounts are available (please call us)

Shipping and handling are included in these prices. (For priority mail, please add $2.00 per book to the above prices.)

Name: _____

Address: _____

City, State, Zip: _____

Phone: _____

Email: _____

Number of books: _____ x $_____ =

Priority Mail (optional): # of books: _____x $2=

Total: _____

Please make checks payable to Prayer Partners With God Publishing.

Mail to: Prayer Partners With God Publishing
            P.O. Box 9292
            Englewood, CO 80111